very truly yours
Josie Washburn

The
Underworld Sewer

A Prostitute Reflects on Life in the Trade, 1871–1909

By
JOSIE WASHBURN

Introduction to the Bison Books Edition
by Sharon E. Wood

UNIVERSITY OF NEBRASKA PRESS

LINCOLN AND LONDON

Introduction © 1997 by the University of Nebraska
Press
All right reserved
Manufactured in the United States of America

⊗ The paper in this book meets the minimum
requirements of American National Standard for
Information Sciences—Permanence of Paper for
Printed Library Materials, ANSI Z39.48-1984.

First Bison Books printing: 1997

Library of Congress Cataloging-in-Publication Data
Washburn, Josie, 1853–
The underworld sewer: a prostitute reflects on life in
the trade, 1871–1909 / by Josie Washburn: introduction to the Bison Books edition by Sharon E. Wood.
p.   cm.
Originally published: Omaha: Washburn Pub. Co.,
1909.
Includes bibliographical references.
ISBN 0-8032-9797-1 (alk. paper)
1. Prostitution—United States—History—19th
century. I. Title.
HQ144.W3   1998   97-18232
306.74'0973'09034—dc21   CIP

Reprinted from the original 1909 edition by the
Washburn Publishing Company, Omaha, Nebraska.

INTRODUCTION

Sharon E. Wood

A LIFE IN THE TRADE

A girl or woman who comes to the underworld institution must undergo a long siege of experience before she is able to understand the underworld.

—Josie Washburn

Josie Washburn underwent her own long siege in the underworld before she emerged in 1907 to write and publish a book about it. *The Underworld Sewer* is that rarest of documents: a reflection on prostitution in the nineteenth-century United States by a woman who lived as a prostitute. It is not autobiography, although it contains autobiographical elements. Nor is it an evangelical tract written for the social purity movement.[1] Instead, *The Underworld Sewer* is a critical analysis of brothel prostitution written in the sure and angry voice of experience.

Authentic writings by prostitutes from the nineteenth century are few. The woman known as "Mamie Pinzer," whose letters to reformer Fanny Quincy Howe are now held at the Schlesinger Library, began working as a casual prostitute around the turn of the century and wrote her letters between 1910 and 1922. An autobiography, *Madeleine*, published anonymously in 1919 and covering a career in prostitution that ended almost twenty years earlier, appears to blend memory with fiction, but its author has not been identified nor her story verified.[2]

Josie Washburn, however, wrote and published her book within two years of leaving life as a prostitute, and evidence of her career is abundant in the historical record. Her name may be found in court records, in city directories, in the manuscript census, in newspapers, and in a letter remaining from the correspondence she formed with the director of the Nebraska State Historical Society, A. E. Sheldon, when she donated the book and pamphlets she published. From these it is possible to piece together a version of her life, but it is a narrative of gaps, silences, and mysteries. Many of these mysteries are of Washburn's own making, strategies she adopted as she moved between identities—one associated with the underworld, and one with her efforts to live a respectable life. The woman who tries to reform carries a peculiar burden, Washburn asserted. "Every minute of her past holds a secret; they are her unwelcome companions" (291).

Josie Washburn was born probably around 1853, in Rhode Island, or Maine, or Wisconsin, to parents who were natives of Scotland, or Maine, or Norway. Or she may have been born somewhere else, to parents of yet another ancestry. Her name then was not Josie, but may have been Helena. Like many prostitutes, Washburn used at least one pseudonym in her work and created various false histories to go with it. The stories were part of the fantasy created for men, as well as a means of maintaining self-respect. "It is a well known fact that men who mingle with us deceive and lie to us," wrote Washburn, "therefore the girls regard it as fair play to 'hand them back a bunch'" (43). Over the decades, she shared different versions of her story with the census takers. In 1925, she wrote a brief sketch offering yet another version of her past, which she gave to the Nebraska State Historical Society along with her book. It begins not with her birth, but with the moment she thought most significant, her immersion into the underworld:

> I stumbled into Omaha in August 1871—I was 17 years old[.] After a day or so I found myself in the establishment of Anna Wilson on lower Douglas Street—I have no space to go into details—nor have I a desire—I must be brief—but I will say here that I helped her to accumulate the half million dollars which she left to the different charitable organizations of Omaha—we grew to be friendly—and I remained with her until the summer of 1879.

Anna Wilson, who died in 1911, did indeed leave an estate eventually worth a half-million dollars to the city and charities of Omaha. She was later remembered in local folklore as the "Queen of the Underworld." But in 1871, her brothel in the double house at 136 and 138 Douglas Street was rather modest. The 1870 census shows her living with her long-time partner, the saloonkeeper Daniel Allen, and three young women identified as "shirtmakers," one of whom was African-American. Josie Washburn's business relationship with Anna Wilson lasted eight years, apparently ending in July 1879. After years of appearing almost monthly on prostitution charges before the Omaha Police Court, Washburn's name vanishes from court records. That same month, Josie Washburn shot herself. Newspapers reported the shooting as an accident, a clumsy moment while Washburn was "handling" a revolver.[3] Washburn recovered, but her repeated insistence in later years that suicide was common among prostitutes hints at another explanation for the episode. Washburn herself never mentioned the event in her autobiographical sketch. Instead, she marked that summer with a different memory, marriage.

Washburn's marriage poses yet another set of mysteries. Her husband, she wrote, was "the only son of a distinguished college professor." His name may have been Frank Stone. But no public record of the marriage has come to light, and just where Josie and her husband may have lived from 1880 to 1895 remains unknown. Washburn expected marriage to transform her life. Her husband was not the hack driver or bartender whom a prostitute might expect to meet and marry, but a sojourner from the middle class. Washburn hoped that with love and an "educated husband," her "days of grief and sorrow" would end. Her own feelings, she declared, were "strong enough to lift me high above all my mistakes of the past," and to lead her into "a pure angelic life." But the husband on whom Washburn rested her hopes proved to be a "profligate" and a "degenerate." He abandoned her. "There came a time," wrote Washburn, "when I realized that my life was a blank[,] that he had drifted so far away that he would never return—so down I went again—but not to the bottom." Fifteen years after her marriage, Josie Washburn returned to prostitution, this time as proprietress of her own brothel in Lincoln, Nebraska.

In Lincoln, Washburn and her "boarders"—there were five in 1900—served a clientele drawn from the various classes in Nebraska's capital city. Politicians and conventioneers, visitors to the state fair, businessmen, church members, German immigrants, American travelers, and students at the University of Nebraska all found their way to the parlors and bedrooms at 226 South Ninth Street. And as Washburn insistently pointed out, so did the sisters and daughters of such men.

The timing of Washburn's return to the underworld is suggestive. In 1893, the nation tumbled into a severe economic depression. High unemployment sent men tramping in search of work, only to find that conditions in one town were as bad as in another. Women, especially those made desperate by the unemployment—or disappearance—of a husband or father, faced dismal competition in the few legitimate occupations open to most women: domestic service, sewing, and unskilled manufacturing jobs. When factories shut down and ladies dismissed their household help, prostitution might emerge as a reasonable option for the unemployed. Did Washburn's faltering marriage crumble under the pressure of unemployment? Did she return to the underworld only after failing to find other work? How many of the women who worked in her house made the choice under the pressure of family poverty and desperation? The tide of economic upheaval that fellow Nebraskan William Jennings Bryan rode to national prominence in 1896 may have swept Josie Washburn back into the underworld barely a year earlier.

Washburn kept her brothel in Lincoln for twelve years. She quit the business in 1907 and moved to Omaha, arriving just in time to witness a high-stakes political conflict over prostitution in that city. The conflict, which began to unfold in December 1907, forms the basis of Washburn's chapter "The One-Year War." Once again, the timing is suggestive. Perhaps Washburn always planned to write a book after leaving the business, or perhaps reading daily newspaper reports that failed to evoke the misery and exploitation of prostitutes ignited her fury and helped her find her voice. In 1909, *The Underworld Sewer* became the first product of the Washburn Publishing Co., which Josie later acknowledged "contained only myself." It also published two pamphlets based on chapters of her book: *The Scourge of Civilization: A Dangerous Disease not Mentioned* (1913), on venereal disease, and *The First Drink, Saloon and Dance Hall* (1914).

Details of Washburn's next years are sketchy. In 1911, she proposed a bill to the Nebraska legislature asking $100,000 for an institution to assist prostitutes who wished to reform—a suggestion she first set out in the closing chapter of her book. She also formed a friendship with Hester Tuttle Griffith, a Minnesota native living in Hollywood, California. How Washburn and Griffith became acquainted is another mystery, though it probably came about through the circulation of *The Underworld Sewer*. Griffith had a long career as an activist in the Woman's Christian Temperance Union, one of the most effective political groups concerned with prostitution. Washburn dedicated her 1914 pamphlet on saloons and dance halls "To My Friend, Mrs. Hester T. Griffith, who helped to bring about Women's Suffrage in the State of California."[4]

By 1920 Washburn had moved to Minneapolis, perhaps with the encouragement of Hester Griffith, who
had grown up in Minnesota. In her new home, she took
up a conventional business for an aging woman; she operated a boarding house—a business that may have
drawn rather neatly on skills she learned running a
brothel. In August 1925, Washburn wrote to A. E. Sheldon
at the Nebraska State Historical Society, mentioning
her plan to move to Spokane that fall to make her home
with a niece. Washburn disappears from Minneapolis
that year, but she does not reappear in Spokane—at least
not in the surviving records. She would have been past
seventy in 1925; where she lived out the end of her life
is one final mystery.

THE SEWER AND ITS DENIZENS

We are there because we must have bread. The
man is there because he must have pleasure; he
has no other necessity for being there; true,
if we were not there the men would not come.
But we are not permitted to be anywhere else.

At first glance, "the underworld sewer" seems a merely
sensational title, borrowed—like the use of capital letters for emphasis—from the tracts of anti-prostitution
societies. But while Josie Washburn may have been an
amateur publisher, she was a thoughtful writer, with a
knack for the apt image. A sewer, after all, is not a bad
thing. One might not want to spend time there, but one
would not want to live in a city without one, either.
And that is Washburn's point. If the underworld func-

tions as a "sewer," protecting respectable women by helping "to drain the impurities of the Christian world" (20), then the women who work there ought to be treated "with kindness and consideration," in gratitude "for the sacrifice [they] are making" (21–23). To make them outcasts is the worst hypocrisy.

Washburn never concedes that prostitution is necessary, but she directs a clear, critical eye on the results of a system that demands the services of prostitutes while declaring them pariahs. With no claim to the protection of law, women of the underworld were easy targets for police graft, greedy landlords, and ambitious politicians. In "The Hold-Up," for example, Washburn lays out the different schemes of policing under which her Lincoln brothel operated—schemes familiar to historians because they were used in cities all over the country. From the prostitutes' point of view, these ranged from the "humane" system of fines paid by messenger to the public humiliation of "the raid." Washburn also uses the power of the press—her own press—to claim the last word in a court case: the 1906 prosecution of former Lincoln police chief Olin Routzahn and city detective William Bentley for blackmailing Washburn and six other brothelkeepers. The women provided the primary evidence in the prosecution, but the men were acquitted on all counts. Washburn lashes out against a system that disregards the testimony of prostitutes, but never questions that of the men who visit them—or become wealthy off their trade.[5]

In "The Man-Landlady" and "The One-Year War," Josie Washburn turns her critical gaze on the wealthy and powerful men who preyed on Omaha's prostitutes.

She has special contempt for the Man-Landlady—in this case M. F. Martin, who owned not only the alley cribs she describes, but perhaps a dozen more brothels as well—because he has become rich from "soul traffic . . . when all the avenues to respectable and honorable business have been open to him" (51). He stands in contrast to the women like herself who run brothels "because they have no other homes, and because they are absolutely cut off from the world; they can see no other choice" (51). The King Gambler described in "The One-Year War" was Omaha political boss Tom Dennison, who built his machine on the vice district of the Third Ward, backed by the *Omaha Bee* (thinly veiled as the "B").[6] In tracing the web of corruption that enveloped the women of Omaha's underworld, Washburn argues that campaigns against vice never succeed because they are never meant to succeed. Too many men derive wealth and political influence from prostitution to willingly end it. Her contempt for these men echoes in her calls for the political and economic empowerment of women:

> You will not fully appreciate the situation, or fairly understand why it is that the social evil exists . . . unless you will be willing to keep in mind while reading its history that men (not women) make and repeal the laws; that men enforce the laws or render the laws dead letters, as suits their desires; . . . that men, not women, determine what opportunities the girl shall have for escaping the pitfalls and emergencies, while driving them to the underworld. (54)

Her call for women's suffrage is direct and explicit, and it places her squarely in the mainstream of Progressive Era advocates of votes for women. Voting women, they hoped, would end the corruption of bosses like Dennison.

Men like Dennison and Martin are not the only ones who draw Washburn's wrath. She takes aim at the "vampire" who victimizes the prostitute by playing to her loneliness and winning her love. In some cases, he takes her money, and "to remind her of the depth of his love, . . . he punches her in the eye ever so often" (144). And not all lovers, she asserts, come from the lower classes. "The most numerous lover in the underworld is the respectable man, in a respectable business" (147). Men like these know where "to obtain a financial lift in a pinch; this has been the making of many a rich man" (148).

Washburn writes about these "vampire lovers" in general terms, but she is generalizing from personal experience. In 1900, while she was keeping her brothel in Lincoln, Washburn sued Fred Nagel for breach of promise to marry her, and for repayment of almost four thousand dollars in loans, made between 1897 and 1899. Nagel had purchased a small paper, the *Freie Presse*, in 1896 and was in the process of building it into a nationally read newspaper with a circulation of 140,000—apparently with Josie Washburn's money. After accepting the loans, Nagel married someone else. Washburn lost her suits, and probably her money. Her former employer, Anna Wilson, apparently had better business sense. Some of Omaha's most prominent citizens turned to the "Queen of the Underworld" for loans. Among those who owed Wilson money at the time of her death were real estate developer Dan Shull; attorney N. H. Loomis, general solicitor for the Union Pacific Railroad; grain mer-

chant George C. Johnson; Peter Iler's Omaha Brick and
Tile Co.; and the city's oldest and most prestigious social organization, the Omaha Club.[7]

THE WOMEN OF THE UNDERWORLD

> The girls you meet in the hallways, the parlors, every-
> where, are of different types of beauty, but a close ob-
> server will behold the stamp upon their different fea-
> tures of bewilderment, fear, unutterable sadness,
> resignation, dread, defiance and despair. The wonder
> is how a system can exist so calloused as to consign
> them to such a life.

In dedicating her book to "the people of village, city,
state, and nation" who "maintain the social evil," Josie
Washburn sets out her purpose in writing it: to impli-
cate her readers in the maintenance of the underworld,
and to move them to action. Yet for those who read her
book, much of its fascination may lie in Washburn's
authority to report the lives of "the girls you meet in
the hallways," her colleagues and employees in the trade.

Like the prostitutes in social purity tracts, the women
who populate Washburn's underworld are victims. They
come to their fate "by two broad ways, men's double
dealing, deception, and lust; and by deprivation, poverty, and abuse" (107). Here are infatuated girls abandoned by their lovers. Here are wives discarded by their
husbands, and daughters struggling to support dependent parents. The man who robs a woman of her "reputation" (never her "honor") is filled with "sexual cravings
and lust," but the woman seems untouched by desire.
Sexuality for her is a "sacrifice," an act of obedience by

one "dazzled and beguiled." Since the beginning of time, a "woman never lived who was bold enough to make the first advance to a man" (105).

That Washburn chooses to portray prostitutes this way is no surprise. Even if bold women or lustful girls made the first advance, Washburn's point is that only women suffer economic consequences. By moving women's sexuality out of the realm of discussion, Washburn focuses attention on what to her is the real issue, the economic and political structures that drive women to the underworld and profit from them once they are there. By the same strategy, she refuses to capitulate to one conventional explanation for prostitution: that women become prostitutes to satisfy their own unnatural lusts.

The women of Washburn's underworld may be conventional in their sexual passivity, but in other ways they are a surprisingly diverse group. They are vulgar and devious, generous and frightened, proud and despairing. Some are utterly cynical, and some are romantic fools who enslave themselves to pimps. Indeed, Washburn's effort to understand why women accept beatings from pimps who steal their money is thoughtful and strangely familiar. "The life she is leading has deprived her of the will power to escape, or even the desire to do so. Energy has become diseased or paralyzed, and she is in a pitiful state which is only possible to surmount by medical and moral applications," explains Washburn (146), sounding very much like a psychologist describing "battered-wife syndrome."

This loss of will is only one of the results Washburn reports for those who remain in the life. After a year,

Washburn argues, a woman "either becomes a tough, hardened creature who is always ready to take a part in every kind of depravity, or is stupefied with dope, lovers and more dope. Or else she is awakened to the horrors of her plight and makes every plan to extricate herself therefrom" (328). Washburn passes lightly over the details of depravity (she rightly feared prosecution under the Comstock Law), but her description of a prostitute smoking opium with an eccentric "society gentleman" is vivid and explicit.[8]

Washburn also returns often to the theme of how difficult it is for a woman to leave the life—and as one who tried at least twice, she had reason to know. To succeed, a woman must be willing to "slave for small wages," and she must guard her past against detection. "It is not possible to tell the truth about herself and receive the respect which she knows she is entitled to," so she lies, replacing one sin with another (290–91). Low wages, the impossibility of providing references, reformers who "talk twaddle" and are "inferior in intellect"—all of these hinder the woman who would reform. One person who does not hinder her is her madam.

Having been a madam herself, Washburn is notably sensitive to the cruelties alleged to the "landlady of the underworld." Her chapter on "The Madam" sets forth with some pride the virtues of the "wise matron" who is "a woman of many resources and sound judgment" (177). She mediates disputes, protects girls from exploitation by pimps, steers them clear of "dope fiends" and "good-for-nothings," and above all does not keep her girls prisoners—as was often asserted. The house, like a department store, is a business and must make a profit. The madam, like the girls, is trapped, knowing "the world would soon give her the 'cold shoulder' if she did not have the money to pay her way" (186).

In the summer of 1925, when she was past seventy, Josie Washburn sat down and typed out a brief history of her life. She sent it, with her book, to the Nebraska State Historical Society. In these acts, Josie Washburn recognized what it would take many decades for historians in universities to understand: that the life of a prostitute is a matter of history. She looked over her book with a critical eye, and found it wanting. "While I could re-write it now and eliminate the clumsiness of my effort—and tell some cold facts in suitable words—I find after these many years of retirement—the subject is so repugnant to me that I cannot take it up again." Readers today may regret her choice, may wish that she had written more, telling "cold facts in suitable words." But we can be grateful for her courage. It must have taken courage for a woman so careful to veil her past in mysteries to write a book about it—and to "scatter" that book "pretty much all over the United States and in Canada and England." And we can admire the pride that made her leave her book to history—and to us.

NOTES

I am grateful to Karrie L. Cole of the Nebraska State Historical Society for her invaluable assistance in researching this introduction.

1. "Social purity" refers to a collection of reforms pursued by various groups in the last third of the nineteenth century,

all of them concerned with sexual conduct. Anti-prostitution campaigns were part of the social purity movement, as were efforts to ban pornography and contraceptive devices. Not everyone who supported one aspect of "social purity" supported all the goals associated with the term.

2. Mamie Pinzer, *The Mamie Papers* (Old Westbury NY: Feminist Press, 1977); *Madeleine: An Autobiography* (New York: Harper and Brothers, 1919; reprint, New York: Persea Books, 1986).

3. Reports of the shooting incident appeared in *Omaha Daily Bee* 18 July 1879, p. 4, and *Omaha Herald* 18 July 1879, p. 8.

4. *Steinauer Star* 16 February 1911, p. 1; *Woman's Who's Who of America*, 1914–1915 (New York: American Commonwealth, 1914), 345.

5. *State of Nebraska* v. *Olin M. Routzahn et al.*, 81 Nebraska 133.

6. John Kyle Davis, "The Gray Wolf: Tom Dennison of Omaha," *Nebraska History* 58 (spring 1977): 25–52; Orville D. Menard, *Political Bossism in Mid-America: Tom Dennison's Omaha, 1900–1933* (Lanham MD: University Press of America, 1989).

7. *Evening State Journal* (Lincoln NE) 24 August 1940, p. 1; *Lincoln Evening News* 8 February 1901, p. 6; Inventory, in the matter of the estate of Anna Wilson, County Court, Douglas County, Nebraska, vol. 93, p. 707.

8. The Comstock Law (An Act for the Suppression of Trade in, and Circulation of Obscene Literature and Articles of Immoral Use) was passed by Congress in 1873 at the urging of Anthony Comstock, head of a New York anti-vice society. It was invoked against a wide range of books and printed materials, including the prostitute's autobiography, *Madeleine*, mentioned above. Its original publisher was convicted and withdrew the book.

TO
THE PEOPLE OF
VILLAGE, CITY, STATE AND
NATION, WHICH BOTH CONSCIOUSLY
AND UNCONSCIOUSLY MAINTAIN THE SOCIAL EVIL,
THIS BOOK IS
DEDICATED.

CONTENTS.

ILLUSTRATIONS.

Preface

The social evil presents the most serious question that comes under the modern limelight. And unless there shall be radical changes in the methods of dealing with this seething undercurrent of abomination, which is increasing at a most rapid rate, the nation may be engulfed.

An honest and candid investigation will raise the curtain higher than I have dared to do, and make a full exposure which will prove that my statements are rendered comparatively mild.

It is not my intention to condemn good men and women, but to awaken them to some awful facts. It is my hope that when they shall be so wakened, that they will boldly and vigorously enlist in the cause of abolishing the evil, not by tyranny over and abuse of my unfortunate sister, but by each individual becoming inspired to examine his or her thought upon the subject of our deplorable condition, and contribute such *sane* remedies as the colossal evil demands, and to help sweep away the present system with its social evil establishments everywhere.

It is the purpose of this book to furnish such information as will cause the people of the nation to realize that they are plodding along the old, old lines, without any good results.

I make no claim to literary attainments, but have undertaken to give some true and necessary glimpses of life in the UNDERWORLD SEWER, in plain language not offensive to the ear of any practical and thoughtful person.

If some good shall come to womankind as the result of my effort, I will be thankful that I have undertaken the work.

JOSIE WASHBURN.

CHAPTER I.

The Evil

The social evil presents the most important question that can arise, in the government of any family, neighborhood, village, city, state or nation.

When you contemplate the sorrow, disgrace and degradation it brings to humanity, you give it up and decide—that, "it is a necessary evil."

It is most wonderful, and unnatural that all classes of people in civilized nations expressly or tacitly agree that the social evil can not be overcome or abolished, but that it is "a necessary evil" which must be tolerated, and possibly regulated.

You need not look beyond the boundaries of the United States for the purpose of

The Underworld Sewer

learning that the social evil is undermining
the foundation of our governments and
bringing to humanity the most dangerous
and shocking diseases, misery and sin.

He will not admit that the evil is of such
great necessity that he will willingly sacrifice one of his own daughters to the cause.

The wise father or mother of a family of
boys and girls is in control of their home.

A father of respectability will never for
one moment allow this evil to exist in his
household.

In case they find the evil appearing in any
form they do not admit that it is a "necessary evil"; or that one or more of their girls
must be sacrificed in order that the others
may live pure lives.

Wise parents who discover a condition in
their home which tends to bring about this
evil, immediately change the condition, and
accomplish the result.

That which is good and can be successfully accomplished in one family may be
accomplished in other families under proper
education and training.

The Evil

It may be said that the best regulated families bring up girls who come to the underworld.

Such is not a correct statement, for it must be acknowledged that there is something wrong in the regulation and condition which, if understood by the parents, might have been avoided or removed.

In other words, if the father and mother of the daughter who comes from, what we call, one of the best regulated families, to the underworld, had known that a certain condition existed at a certain time, they would not have slept until they had changed that condition.

Therefore it becomes necessary for the fathers and mothers to make themselves familiar with the conditions which make the downfall of their daughters a possibility, before they can understand how to prevent the conditions.

The girl who goes wrong is not so much to blame for her sin as those who create or permit the condition.

You are aware that you owe a duty not

The Underworld Sewer

only to YOUR OWN FAMILY but you must realize that, in order to protect your own family, YOU MUST PROTECT ALL FAMILIES.

You must first be convinced that the social evil is NOT necessary.

If you consider that it is necessary you ought in justice to be willing that one of your own daughters or sister be sacrificed, and not always the daughters or sisters of your neighbors.

So long as you believe a sin is necessary to your existence you will not do anything very substantial toward overcoming the evil.

We can not see that it is necessary, that OUR OWN DAUGHTERS or SISTERS should be sacrificed upon the altar, therefore we will do everything we know how to do, to prevent that sacrifice.

But if you admit that it is necessary for the daughters or sisters of your neighbor to be sacrificed, you are not willing to do very much to prevent such a sacrifice.

Our national capital is the private home of the president of the United States and his

The Evil

cabinet officers; also of the senators, congressmen and the judges of the United States supreme court.

In this home of our nation is presented a most sorrowful picture, in the most honorable stations of life, as well as in the lowest depths of degradation.

The District of Columbia, Washington City, is in the exclusive control of our president and our United States senators and representatives in congress.

These officers are selected by the people of the states and territories as being the most capable men of this enlightened age.

Why is it that such noble men will create or tolerate a condition in that city which entices, ensnares and entraps in all vicious ways, thousands of the best and purest of women, from every state in the union, and bind them in chains of necessity, helplessness and disgrace? It is in the power of these most honorable officers to change these conditions in Washington so that the city would stand as a living monument and demonstration and as an example for other cities, and

11

The Underworld Sewer

for other nations, showing that a city CAN exist and prosper without the social evil.

Is it worth while to consider the reason why such a condition exists, and what remedy may be successfully applied?

It is just as much in the power of the president and congress to eliminate from its city the social evil as it is for the father and mother of a family to eliminate such evil from their home.

The whole matter depends upon the desire and determination of the president and congress.

Let us inquire! Why will not the president and lawmakers protect the government home?

In my environments I have, for years, been studying the question. I have lost no opportunities to learn the cause and note the effect of this monstrous evil in all its phases.

I know the history of the girl born and raised in poverty and ignorance.

And the girl born in luxury, with education and refinement.

The Evil

I know the life of the clerk in the store and the office girl and servant girl.

I know by experience, association and observation of the temptations which girls meet in the various stages of life.

I know of the offers of assistance and the conditions growing therefrom.

I know of the sorrow and yieldings and of the many paths on the downward road.

I know of the resolutions and efforts to retrace the step and I know of the cold and disinterested world and its cruel rebuffs.

In all these I am informed; and more, I am educated and experienced. For twenty years or more I was either an inmate or a matron of a public house.

But in all that time I have never seen a day in which I was not planning for my deliverance from the life, and trusting that I might be able to do some good in the way of helping others out, and aiding in establishing a condition which would prevent the thousands of good girls and women from being driven or enticed into this most degraded of all horrible lives.

13

The Underworld Sewer

I would much prefer to not relate my own experience, and I do so only for the purpose that you may understand that I know many things in connection with this subject with which you can have but a faint idea.

You do not have to be convinced that the evil is here and that it is very, VERY bad, but you do not realize the danger which it brings to your family, your neighborhood, your village, your city, your state, and your nation.

History repeats itself, and in the downfall of nations both ancient and modern the social evil has been behind the scenes, the first and greatest cause.

The history of the social evil, ancient or modern, proves that all methods which have heretofore been adopted relating to the evil have been and are absolute failures.

It is also plain that such methods could not possibly be anything but failures.

And I suspect were not intended to be anything but failures.

These same old remedies are applied, first one and then another, in different genera-

The Evil

tions and different times, but only to be handled in the same old way, which has proven worthless throughout history.

In all countries this monster has been recognized as a necessity and is at present recognized by each and every civilized nation of the present day as a necessity.

Think for a moment—is the social evil truly a necessary evil in our nation?

If so, WHY is it necessary?

If not, then the most important step is to realize that it IS NOT a necessary evil.

When the great producing cause of the social evil shall be recognized and admitted, then the proper methods to be adopted for the eradication of the same will appear.

It is said by scholars that there was no social evil known to the human race until civilization was introduced, and it is said that there are tribes at the present time in which there is no knowledge of civilized life wherein this evil is unknown.

History of the middle ages informs us that this evil was maintained by the government and that the women engaged were compelled

The Underworld Sewer

to pay a percentage of their earnings to the CHURCH.

In this enlightened age their money is not applied to church purposes directly. But it is taken from them under the guise of a fine or license, by virtue of law, and applied to the education of the children, which I suppose is considered by our lawmakers as a better cause than the church, and an improvement, in the manner of taking their money, than that adopted in the middle ages.

In our day the government takes our money, but does not take care of the women and give them a home as was done in ancient times. In effect the system is practically the same, but in our day the system is less humane.

Free women of the old Greeks and Romans whose purity was questioned were made outcasts, beyond all redemption, and they, together with the slave women, were subjected to the brutal lust of men, with no disgrace to the men.

It seems to be about the same, as a practical proposition, in the present age. Can you see any difference?

The Evil

THE MODERN SYSTEM IS A PRETENSE of lawful control of the evil.

The modern system is founded upon the basis that this evil is necessary for the safety of the community.

But the system pretends at times to try to ERADICATE THAT WHICH IT SAYS IS A NECESSITY.

The system calls itself regulation of evil.

The system stands for inconsistency, lack of principle and insincerity.

The system stands for avarice, tyranny, viciousness, crime, degradation and death.

The system of regulation stands for fraud and corruption.

The system stands for oppression and graft.

The system of REGULATION REQUIRES THAT THE REGULATORS BE THOSE ONLY WHO WANT THE EVIL TO CONTINUE.

The system of regulation STANDS FOR DRIVING OUR PEOPLE LIKE RATS, from one locality to another.

The effect of this driving process only

17

The Underworld Sewer

means more misery to the helpless and the shifting of the burden upon the people of a different locality.

Our system has the support of good citizens, of scholars, of students, and of the church. It has the support of the lawmakers, and law officers.

Why should you tolerate or support a system which says that the men may INSIST but the woman must RESIST?

Why should it be said that a man may be a GENTLEMAN and yet PROPOSE, SUGGEST, HIRE and tempt the women in all ways; but that the girl must, in her helpless inexperience, resist or forever be disgraced.

CHAPTER II.

Is It Necessary?

Is social evil necessary as a protection for respectable women and girls against violent and brutish attacks of men?

Does the presence of the public women, with whom men may associate, obviate the crime of rape in the community where such women carry on their business?

In other words, is the public house necessary in order to satisfy men who otherwise would outrage respectable girls and women?

In all stages of civilized life it has been maintained by men and women that there would be no end to criminal assaults, rapine and murder of good women and girls if there were no public women.

It is not so important how this sentiment has been in ancient times, or how it is in foreign countries.

19

The Underworld Sewer

But it is most important to know what the current belief is upon this point, in our own country as a nation, as a state, or as a city.

If such is the sentiment prevailing with our people as a general rule, then the minds of our people must be educated and trained in a different channel before any great change can take place.

Must a part of the girls and women of our nation, state, city, village, or family, be offered as a sacrifice, and be cast into everlasting darkness and despair, in order that other girls and women may live in safety, happiness, comfort, luxury, respectability and finally enter the heavenly gates?

If such is to be the acknowledged system in our civilization then why should an effort be made to redeem those who have already become a sacrifice to the cause?

If the underworld is the sewer through which to drain the impurities from the Christian world, why recall those who have started? Is it to make room for others?

If you will read the reports of eminent citizens, men of learning, who have of late

Is It Necessary?

years studied the situation, you find that there is a strong belief that the men of the human family are as far from self control in the present day as they have been in all history and THAT THERE WOULD BE A GREAT FLOOD of crimes, and assaults upon our respectable sisters if THERE SHOULD BE NO PUBLIC WOMEN WITH WHOM MEN COULD ASSOCIATE LAWFULLY.

Therefore the conclusions are that it is not wise to suppress the social evil, even if it be possible.

If this sentiment is correct and the keeping of public women for such purposes is necessary as a PROTECTION FOR OTHER GIRLS AND WOMEN, then the unfortunate sister SHOULD BE TREATED WITH KINDNESS AND CONSIDERATION; it would be right for the state or nation to do as they did in olden times, that is, support and care for them so that they might the better fill their mission.

Those who are in favor of maintaining

The Underworld Sewer

this slavery justify themselves with this same old excuse, that it is necessary in order that our wives and daughters may be safe upon the streets. Oh, no! They don't make speeches in campaigns as plain as that! They don't preach in their pulpits as plain as that!

BUT THEY GO INTO THE VOT-ING BOOTH AND CAST THEIR VOTES in SUPPORT of SUSTAIN-ING the INSTITUTION which does double service, in that it PROTECTS THE GOOD WOMEN, and ENTER-TAINS THE BAD MAN.

The ballot always speaks louder than words.

When you vote for an administration that will permit the evil in the city as a necessity, you ought to go further and protect those WHO MAKE THE SACRIFICE for the safety of your wives and daughters.

You should provide that they shall not be abused, like slaves, by your brothers, your cousins, your uncles, your sons and your fathers, who would otherwise commit crimi-

Is It Necessary?

nal assault upon respectable girls and women except for the sacrifice our women are making.

In such case you ought to go still further. You ought to so GUARD and protect these women who make this GREAT sacrifice for the protection of their good sisters against the assault of the villainous men, that they would not be OBLIGED TO SUFFER FROM COLD AND HUNGER, or be COMPELLED to ACCEPT THE SMALLEST PIECE of money in exchange for their souls.

You vote for an administration to perpetuate the evil because the good sister needs protection, the men need the evil association, and the merchant, the saloon, and the police department need the money which the social evil supporter puts in circulation.

The truth is that this evil which you regard as a protection to good women, IS NO PROTECTION AT ALL.

I hope to convince you that such an idea has no foundation.

For the present let me call your attention

The Underworld Sewer

to just one blunt fact, which you can prove for yourself.

Take under consideration two cities of the same number of population, in the same latitude, and a similar citizenship as to nationalities.

In one of these cities for a course of years no public house is permitted or tolerated; in the other city public houses are allowed and encouraged in the manner and form as they are allowed to carry on the business.

Now having selected your cities, look up the record and you will find there has been many more criminal assaults upon girls and women in the city where the public houses are allowed than there is in the city where they are not allowed.

A careful estimate will show that the more there is of the social evil in a city, regulated or not regulated, no difference which, the greater the criminal assault and kindred crimes.

This one fact well considered will end the contention that the social evil is necessary as a protection to the public.

Is It Necessary?

When you hear a man say that the social evil is a necessary evil for the protection of good women, just put it down that the man is one of those who wants the public house in his city for other reasons than the safety of good women.

It may be for financial, political or other reasons which he does not like to state. When you hear a woman say it is necessary for the safety of good women, pity her on account of her ignorant stupidity.

I dare say where you find a village, town or city without any women of this character many years will pass by without a criminal assault being made.

It is not a question of importance whether you believe this thing, or you pretend to believe it, but that you are deceiving yourself and others by giving out this as a reason for maintaining the social evil, as a protection against criminal assault of brutal men, when in fact the greater the number of criminal assaults, houses of that character are greater in proportion. "Evil begets evil."

25

The Underworld Sewer

"Vice is a monster of so frightful mien,
As to be hated, needs but to be seen;
Yet seen too oft, familiar with her face,
We first endure, then pity, then embrace."

CHAPTER III.

The Hold=Up

For twelve years I was a matron of a public house in Lincoln, Nebraska.

This city has a population of over sixty thousand. It is a city of colleges and churches and is as moral and well conducted as any you will find.

There are fewer houses of this character in this city than any of a like population within my knowledge. I left there in May, 1907. Not because I was obliged to do so; any complaint regarding my business could have been adjusted as it had been many times before.

I had for several years planned to quit in 1907 and to take up the work I am now doing—throwing the searchlight on the underworld.

During the time I resided in Lincoln the

The Underworld Sewer

number of "houses" ranged from a half
dozen to a dozen, of different grades. They
were not of the extremely fashionable kind
with costly furniture, nor of the lowest
grade such as you will find in larger cities.

As in all cities there were factions in politics which took turns in governing the city
and which were always at war with each
other.

The football of contention was the underworld. They often exposed each other and
each faction charged the other with misde-
meanors and crime of some sort, and the
charges were usually sustained by the facts.

One of the most profitable grafts was the
money they drew from the unfortunate
women of the city.

During the twelve years that I was in
"business" there I paid a monthly fine of
from $14.70 up to $29.70. The girls paid
from $5.70 to $9.70 each month.

Administrations had different methods of
governing us, which means different ways of
taking our money from us. Some would
permit us to make a list of the names and

The Hold-Up

the amount and send it up by a messenger. The slip came back marked O. K.

This was the humane way.

The next one would compel us to come up to headquarters and each one pay her own fine, that they might see us and know us and keep tab on us.

This was a coarse and brutal way.

We always went with fear and trembling.

Two officers or more would be appointed to get the inmates of one house and when they had "settled" and gone the same officers would get another "herd," and so on until all had paid. Those who did not have the money were thrown into jail until someone paid the bill, or it was otherwise arranged with the police.

At other times, semi-occasionally, it was deemed necessary to make a favorable impression upon the good citizen of the city; or the "powers" needed extra money on the side. Then the authorities would not give us any notice at all, but would swoop down upon us and make a raid. In that case they

The Underworld Sewer

would pile us all in the wagon like a lot of criminals, and carry us through the streets.

Oh, the grief! the disgrace! the tears! the wounded pride! Some of the women would throw scarfs over their heads and faces, to keep from being seen.

To the warped minds who believe that a fallen woman is incapable of possessing a human emotion, it would be useless to explain our feelings, but those who are less burdened with ignorance and prejudice regarding us will have a faint comprehension of our sufferings when I say that each time we were taken up in that way we felt like committing suicide.

Raids are for the purpose of making a show to the public, or to force the women to submit to graft.

We regarded this treatment as unjust and cruel, but the effect was to make us more willing to part with our cash.

At times the fines would cease, but they would get the same amount of money out of us in some other way. They would order us to sell no beer, knowing well that we depended upon the profit of the same to a

The Hold-Up

great extent for our maintenance, and that we would take chances.

The beer cost us thirteen cents and the customer would pay a dollar and help shield us from the police.

Often we would be caught selling. Then it would be from $50.00 to $100.00 and costs for the "keeper" and the usual fine for the girls, unless they "sassed"; then they also got $50.00 and costs, or from thirty to ninety days in jail.

Under some pretext or another they got our money just the same.

Of course, it was plain to us that by these raids they expected to make a strong impression on the citizen who held the ballot.

The experience of being "held up" by officers of the law is of frequent occurrence in the underworld.

My experience is rendered mild compared to the experience in other cities. For mildness and mercy Lincoln has all other cities "bested" by far.

It was in the years of 1903 and 1904. The administration started us in by a monthly

The Underworld Sewer

fine of $29.70, including costs. We were notified of the amount we were expected to pay. We remonstrated, explaining that there would be nothing left for us to live on.

In order to encourage us to be more reconciled to our fate the officers told us that we could sell beer.

In about two months they came and told us THEY HAD NEVER GIVEN US ANY SUCH P R I V I L E G E AND THAT WE COULD NOT SELL IT, AND IF WE DID WE WOULD BE PUNISHED ACCORDINGLY.

A woman in the underworld will take all kinds of chances when her living depends upon it, all of which the police well know.

We also knew that they would catch us frequently. It wasn't the beer selling they were interested in as much as the catching.

They planned that the oftener they could catch us the more we would be willing to pay for not being caught.

This is the way we managed it: Before we would answer a "ring" every bottle and every glass would be out of sight. If it

The Hold-Up

proved to be a customer we produced our bottles and glasses, and if it was the police there was no evidence against us. Sometimes the atmosphere was so intensely serene and harmless that they took us anyway on general principle and suspicion.

The only thing we could do was to take our medicine, and the dose was usually "one hundred dollars and costs."

It is worse than folly for a woman in the underworld to expect justice and a square deal from the police department, even when there is one due her.

Our women neither expect nor get sympathy from anywhere and must abide by whatever the police require, regardless of law or justice.

Between these fines and these raids we had to make our living the best we could.

During the autumn of the first year of this particular administration public sentiment became strong against the fines, and as time went on it grew stronger. They were finally compelled to drop the fine system. The church element claimed that we paid

The Underworld Sewer

for a privilege in advance. Then the authorities tried to get around the objection by switching our fine day to the end of the month. But it did not work. They were up against it and had to quit. Their predicament wasn't an easy one. They hated to give up our "easy money" and they could not afford to give up the good will of the people. That they would be wise in their decision we did not question. They could get our money through other channels.

A little later on we were arrested. Beer-selling, keeping a public house and vagrancy were the charges.

One hundred dollars and cost, the result.

In answer to an inquiry the police judge warned us that if we came up before him again he might fine us all the way up to five hundred dollars, or possibly give us a jail sentence.

This was plain talk. We understood that we should agree to whatever the police proposed to avoid coming up before the police judge, and we knew the police could take us

The Hold-Up

there at any time and as often as suited their purpose.

Three months or so elapsed and the state fair was on. The fair is always an important event with us. The big profit depends largely upon the disposition of the rulers; whether or not they are friendly enough to give us a chance to make it profitable. As a rule the underworld makes just as much preparations for the fair as others interested do. Girls flock in from adjoining towns and other states. Our houses are full to overflow.

The chief of police and city detective came to demand money September 5, 1904. After carefully scrutinizing the hall and the adjoining room to make sure there were no listeners, they began by apologizing for having had us arrested the last time. Their explanation was that they HAD TO do so.

They said they had been to a lot of expense during the campaign and they were in arrears. They reminded me that we had not paid any fines for a long time. They refreshed my memory as to the warning of

The Underworld Sewer

the police judge's $500.00 and—jail—and
assured me that it would hold good. They
advised me that it would be better to pay
them.

The women in the underworld realize that
they are in the power of the police. They
know these officers, garbed in the authority
of the law, are corruptly taking our money.
Sometimes they conclude to fight, but although truth is on their side they never win
in court. There is no justice for them.

We paid the amount they demanded and
continued to pay these blackmailers our hard
earned money from month to month, as long
as they were in office.

Just before this administration expired
they came to me with this singular and even
comical request, that I work for them during
the campaign in a political way. It does
not require much stretch of the imagination
to guess whether I did or not.

Sometimes an influential woman among
us may obtain favors by doing political
work.

The Hold-Up

This particular hold-up became a matter of public knowledge.

The next administration took possession in the spring of 1905. Of course it was the duty of the new administration to prosecute boodlers and to make political capital for the new executive rulers. The ex-chief and the ex-detective were indicted. After the usual proceedings (to make a long story short), the two ex-officers were found by the jury to be, "Not guilty."

It must have been known to the court and the prosecuting attorney that CERTAIN CITIZENS HAD THE PROPER KNOWLEDGE and information that would support the evidence of the fallen women, and even PROVE THE DEFENDANTS GUILTY WITHOUT THE EVIDENCE OF THE WOMEN. But for some reason they were not sworn or called to testify.

We believe that the prosecution was not intended to convict but only to bring the two ex-officers into disgrace and put them out of the way in politics and at the same time in-

The Underworld Sewer

fuse the public with the idea that the new administration would not be guilty of such grafting.

These cases against the ex-officers created great interest in the public mind. They had practically the same transaction with four other keepers of public houses; five of us were required to appear as witnesses against the two ex's.

It was well known by several citizens who were not called to testify that our money was distributed, A M O N G O F F I C E R S "HIGHER UP." And to protect themselves, they were obliged to protect the two ex-officers.

The trial came on, but there were no witnesses except the five victims.

The evidence was positive and to the point.

Every disinterested person was convinced of their guilt, beyond the possibility of a doubt.

The court, the jury, and the lawyers knew thoroughly well that we testified to the truth AND NOTHING BUT THE TRUTH.

Finally, after all the evidence was in, the

The Hold-Up

court proceeded to instruct the jury, which was in SUBSTANCE AND EFFECT THAT THE DEFENDANTS SHOULD NOT BE CONVICTED OF CRIME BY THE OATH OF FALLEN WOMEN; or rather, his sympathy was with the boodlers and they should not be convicted in his court.

We had no inducement to testify to anything untruthful against these officers, nor could any of us have been influenced to have done so.

The officers were evidently doing what they thought proper.

The new chief and the new detective did not want them convicted, because if officers could be convicted by the testimony of fallen women for boodling, it would make these girls too prominent, and also put a permanent stop to graft.

In the underworld everywhere graft is an important source of revenue, within the reach of all powers.

Any officer can obtain money from the fallen women upon any pretense he pleases,

The Underworld Sewer

with perfect safety AS LONG AS THERE ARE NO WITNESSES TO THE TRANSACTION, E X C E P T FALLEN WOMEN; therefore it is a safe graft, within the reach of grafters.

Let us examine into the question relating to the oath of the fallen women in court.

Why is her testimony under oath not as good and reliable as that of the man who associates with her in the underworld?

One of the charges against us as to truth and veracity, is that we have lost our moral honor.

We cannot understand WHY THAT SHOULD BE COUNTED AGAINST US ANY MORE THAN IT SHOULD BE COUNTED AGAINST MEN OF ALL CLASSES who habitually ASSOCIATE WITH US in our immorality, and SUPPLY THE MONEY which keeps us in the business.

Suppose that one of these men, well known to be such, should be asked by the lawyer on the opposite side, for the purpose of impeaching his oath, the following ques-

The Hold-Up

tion: "Is it not a fact that you habitually associate with fallen women in public houses?" The court in such a case and jury and visitors would be extremely shocked, the lawyer on the side of the witness would object, and the court would rule the question out of order.

The court would say to counsel that "SUCH CONDITION MIGHT BE TRUE, YET THE WITNESS MAY BE A VERY TRUTHFUL MAN, as his reputation for truth and veracity must be impeached in the ordinary way."

But THE FALLEN WOMAN WOULD BE REQUIRED TO ANSWER A QUESTION OF THAT NATURE for the purpose of DISCREDITING HER TESTIMONY.

Is not the man of family who associates with us more dishonorable than we?

The oath of the men who have abandoned their families and every sacred obligation is good in court.

The oath of the men who live by our earnings is not questioned in court.

41

The Underworld Sewer

The oath of the gambler, the ruffian, the reprobate, is taken in court, and no questions asked.

The oath of men who have become wealthy from leasing houses to us is never doubted in court.

In fact, the oath of every man, no matter how depraved, is accepted in court, unless he is put through the impeachment process. WHY IS IT?

There are no good reasons why our oath should not stand good until OUR INDIVIDUAL VERACITY SHOULD BE IMPEACHED in the same manner and form as men are treated.

The fact that our oath is not accepted, subjects us to the grossest insult and injustice and compels us to feel that you are making a mockery of your court of JUSTICE AND THAT IT IS MERELY A RELIC OF BARBARISM.

We are constantly reminded by the police, as well as by all men who abuse us, THAT OUR OATH WILL NOT BE TAKEN IN COURT.

"THE DAUGHTERS, SISTERS AND WIVES OF OTHER MEN"

The Hold-Up

And when we are compelled to give our money to the grafter, WHO HAS THE DROP ON US, we dare not murmur. THERE IS NO RELIEF NOR REMEDY FOR OUR WOMEN.

It is true that our women make no pretense that we tell the truth about our former lives to men who visit us or to slum reformers.

It is a well known fact that men who mingle with us deceive and lie to us, therefore the girls regard it as fair play "to hand them back a bunch," as the occasion seems to require in frivolous affairs.

It is also true that there is no class of people in this country who have so much fear of the penitentiary and punishment in the next world as the fallen women.

It is also true, as a general rule, that OUR WOMEN CANNOT BE INDUCED TO TELL A LIE WHEN UNDER OATH BEFORE A COURT.

I know that the common belief is the other way; but if people could only know how intensely we talk this among ourselves, and

The Underworld Sewer

how we REGARD SWEARING TO A
LIE AS THE GREATEST SIN WE
COULD POSSIBLY COMMIT, then my
statement would appear to be well founded
and true,

CHAPTER IV.

The Man=Landlady

The most despicable member of the underworld is the man-landlady.

There is one in the city of Omaha (where I now reside) who owns the greater share of the red-light district, which is of no small proportions in this city.

This he-landlady leases and controls several alleys, on which he has built rows of cribs, both sides similarly arranged.

Each crib consists of two small rooms, about six feet high; a door and a window forms the whole front. Each crib has a projecting corner, and a casual glance down the line gives it a scalloped appearance, which is meant to be artistic.

These alleys are paved, regardless of expense, and have heavy iron gates at each end. One of these alleys is covered by a fancy

The Underworld Sewer

roof, the ceiling has a showy red design, embellished with many electric lights.

Some of the girls who exist in these alleys are those who have seen years of suffering, and are now addicted to dope and liquor. But the majority are the very young girls who are carried away by the excitement. There is the girl-chum of her own age, there is the din, clatter, and hum of many voices, the bright light, men constantly passing, and at times the alley becomes a surging mass of humanity, all of which has a hypnotic effect upon a young girl.

The cracked electric piano in each crib, all in operation at the same time, sending forth to the jagged men within the inclosure, and also to those outside, such music as seems to them inspiring, and when accompanied by much profanity and obscene language, which appears to ooze from every crevice, acting as a chorus, the victim is also in a hypnotic state, which grows more and more congenial in proportion to the indulgence.

The underworld condition is a boa constrictor, which holds all spellbound; those

The Man-Landlady

who hesitate by the wayside to meddle with it are lost.

These girls who occupy the crib are always under the influence of a lover, who fleeces them of all money above their bare living expenses. Some of these girls with their pretty faces seem so young and frail as to be mere children. Their condition is pathetic in the extreme, as they do not even realize that they are in the worst of slavery.

These girls give no heed to sanitation, not comprehending the necessity to provide for such measures. Consequently diseases of the most malignant and contagious kind are sent broadcast.

There are comparatively no modern improvements in these cribs, except the electric light, with which the place is abundantly supplied.

The only other modern improvement in these cribs is the electric push-button which connects all of them with the saloon on the corner, under which there is a restaurant; these are also owned by this he-landlady, who gets the profit on all food and drinks pur-

The Underworld Sewer

chased at the saloon and restaurant by these girls, and who pay him from one to five dollars daily rent; THIS MUST BE PAID IN ADVANCE, EVERY TWENTY-FOUR HOURS, OTHERWISE THEY ARE MADE TO VACATE BY MOVING THEIR BELONGINGS ON THE STREET.

SUICIDE IS OF FREQUENT OCCURRENCE IN THESE ALLEYS.

From these cribs, and the many big houses, is the deriving source of the monster's great wealth—he who has paid the police and influenced politicians in his behalf for years.

His MONTHLY INCOME from this horrible traffic is several thousand dollars.

He has become very wealthy from the PITIFUL EARNINGS OF HUMAN BEINGS IN DEBAUCHERY.

THERE ARE A NUMBER OF INFLUENTIAL MEN WHO ARE THE OWNERS OF THE TITLE TO THE LAND UPON WHICH THESE CRIBS ARE BUILT, and the OWNERS

The Man-Landlady

of many of THE BIG HOUSES IN THE UNDERWORLD.

They are church members and "desirable" citizens.

Most of the houses in the improved part, as well as the destitute part of the underworld, where the RENTS ARE ENORMOUS, ARE OWNED BY MEN, NOT WOMEN.

Of late there has been GREAT TALK of a "cleaning out" in this section, and the unhappy girls are the cause of the trouble. These frail, diseased, dissipated, wretched girls are pulled out of their miserable cribs by big, strong, bully policemen, who abuse them and use obscenity equal to anything heard in the underworld.

They are the representatives of the law, who are correcting the erring ones.

These weaklings are jerked around by these big brutes and brought before the judge, who takes from them, by way of a fine, THEIR HARD EARNED MONEY, in the name of justice, because some of the politicians have decided to remain in

The Underworld Sewer

office for another term. They must convince
the people of their worthiness; and if the fallen women are only punished hard enough,
public sentiment will be appeased and the
office holder will always be re-elected.

Through the hardship of these girls the
police department is always benefited to the
extent of a lot of money.

The mayor can always POINT WITH
PRIDE TO THE RECORD. The com-
fortable, well fed police judge and city at-
torney GET UP THEIR REPUTA-
TION AS GREAT REFORMERS
AND A TERROR TO VICE.

It is only the crib owner and his tenants
which the city authorities are besieging at
present—it became easy to select him as the
subject upon which to build the necessary
political capital, because he had boasted of
his great income, and it is not to be presumed
that a politician could hear of such wealth
rolling in without having a finger in the pie.

It will be necessary to keep "tab" on affairs for a year, to note the result of the
maneuvers, and to learn if there has been

The Man-Landlady

any improvement on the old time way of dealing with vice.

Upon first thought it may seem unjust that this he-landlady has been singled out as the meanest of human kind, and that he deserves to be confined in the penitentiary for life, but not so when you come to realize that this monster is a rich man, become so from the soul traffic business which he has preferred, when all the avenues to respectable and honorable business life have been open to him.

The women who are running public houses are doing so because they have no other homes, and because they are absolutely cut off from the world; they can see no other choice. With them it is quite a different proposition.

This he-landlady builds houses everywhere that they will be tolerated, having no regard for anybody.

He lives in a magnificent palace in a good part of the city; although EACH BRICK in his palatial home and his enormous prop-

The Underworld Sewer

erties represents a LOST SOUL, he and his household are respected members of society.

This same condition, this he-landlady, who passes as a real estate agent, the same Christian owners of land, and the same persecution of the unfortunate girls, for political and financial purposes, can be found in every city.

CHAPTER V.

The One Year War

A campaign against the social evil is a false pretense conducted by politicians, newspapers, city officials, and the police department for selfish gain in business, politics or graft.

This history is repeated every few years in every city in the United States containing a population of 50,000 or more, and in most cities of smaller size the same farce is played, in a smaller way.

In order that one who reads may call to mind a period of time in his own city, and recognize conditions herein described, this history will not give real names.

The conditions in respect to the social evil are practically the same in all cities of our country which are of about equal population, stupidity, insincerity and ignorance relating to the subject.

The Underworld Sewer

You will not fully appreciate the situation, or fairly understand why it is that the social evil exists, in one form or another, openly or secretly, in some degree, in all parts of our country, nor comprehend with clearness why campaigns against this evil are total failures, unless you will be willing to keep in mind while reading its history that men (not women) make and repeal the laws; that men enforce the laws, or render the laws dead letters, as suit their desires; that men, not women, make the ordinances and rules and regulations for cities, and enforce the same at pleasure; that men conduct the business of the country, and handle the money; that men, not women, determine what opportunities the girl shall have for escaping the pitfalls and emergencies, while driving them into the underworld.

And above all, gentle reader, you will never get on the right road to discover the proper methods to be adopted in order to overcome or suppress the evil until you are willing to recognize the ACTUAL and AWFUL FACT that a very, very great

The One Year War

and overwhelming majority of men of the present day WOULD NOT HAVE THE SOCIAL EVIL ABOLISHED OR SUPPRESSED UPON ANY CONDITIONS, OR UNDER ANY CIRCUMSTANCES.

Small majorities rule if they be in earnest and know how to manage the affairs which confront them.

Just imagine if you can that a majority of men in a village, town, city, state and nation should REALLY and TRULY DESIRE to overcome the evil, and suppose that desire was strong enough in each individual to cause each man to be true and loyal to his pure thoughts; the evil would disappear.

If you will bear in mind the foregoing suggestions, I venture that you will appreciate the history of the "war upon the social evil" in your own town.

One of the objects of this bit of history is to open the eyes of good men and women to the truth relating to the question.

The Underworld Sewer

"Know the truth and the truth will make you free."

The principal characters in the play are:

1st. The women of the underworld, who have no rights under the law upon which they can depend for protection of person or property.

2nd. The monster he-landlady who owns or controls the buildings or shelter where the underworld women carry on their business.

3rd. The king gambler: the political dictator of the lower ward, the go-between for the city official and graft and collectors of campaign funds.

4th. The saloon, which stimulates the men to support and maintain the UNDER-WORLD SEWER.

5th. The NEWSPAPERS, which mould public sentiment, lead political factions, and mislead and deceive well-meaning people upon the subject of the social evil.

6th. The chief of police, who commands the police force and knows which side of his bread is buttered in the management of the police force relating to the social evil.

The One Year War

7th.   The mayor, who is governed in his action by that which seems to insure his re-election, and sometimes by that which pays in advance.

8th.   The police commissioners or board, that has power to appoint and discharge policemen or to direct or govern them.

9th.   The city council, the police officers, the judge of the courts, and the prosecuting attorney are on the stage and all act important parts.

The people constitute the great audience, which look upon the play as a reality.

The lower ward contains the wholesale district, the railroad stations, the banks, the franchised corporations, and other large business interests.

Also the greater number of saloons, gambling dens, and the "Red Light District."

The owners, managers and employers of the great business interests in the lower ward have their homes in OTHER PARTS OF THE CITY.

The thousands of the poorest people, of all colors and nationalities, are crowded into the lower ward.

The Underworld Sewer

They live in old and tumbled down buildings, in cellars, shanties, and anywhere they can find shelter.

The transient, vicious elements make their homes in the lower ward.

This is the ward in which thieves, thugs, burglars, gamblers, pimps, robbers, and illegal voters congregate and thrive.

Every city has its lower ward, and some cities have several of these wards, which are known by different names.

Every city has its newspapers, the Herald, News, and B.

Every city has its king gambler, every city has its he-landlady, and some cities are supplied with many of these slave owners.

The influential citizens in the lower ward are the king gambler and the monster he-landlady of the underworld.

They are the friends of the grafting city officials.

They have great influence in city elections, and campaign managers must count largely as to where that influence will be cast.

And as occasion may require, the news-

The One Year War

papers score them and expose them, or indirectly aid them and uphold them.

These two monstrosities, the he-landlady and the king gambler, are unpopular in the minds of the common people and it is considered to be something of a disgrace upon city officials to be exposed as being mixed up with either of them in the matter of graft.

It is very difficult to see the real object of a newspaper when it opens up a fight against the underworld women; but if one is wise to the situation, one will observe that the real object of the attack is neither to better the condition of the city nor to assist the underworld women.

For several years the Herald has sought to have a new chief of police appointed; a possibility is open; one of the complaints of this daily is that the chief permits assignation houses to do business in the resident districts. This is a fruitful subject upon which to create public sentiment against the chief, and has been agitated by the Herald for some time.

The Underworld Sewer

The following is a clipping from the Herald:

"RESIDENT DISTRICTS MUST BE FREED.

"Chief of Police Has Received Verbal Orders from the Board of Fire and Police Commissioners to Suppress the Social Evil in Residence Districts."

The article continues with a half column, just as though the Herald expected the social evil to be suppressed very suddenly, providing the chief of police would perform his duty.

"MRS. BLACK CONVICTED IN LAKE STREET CASE—CHIEF OF POLICE ON WITNESS STAND.

"Herald Evidence Conclusive and Backed by Testimony of Prominent Citizens.

"Inability to Get Evidence His Explanation for the Protection of This Resort from Complaints."

The head lines a couple of days later are as follows:

The One Year War

"Leavenworth Street
Womán Is Convicted.

"Evidence Conclusive and Defense Introduces No Witnesses—Put Under $250 Bonds."

And followed by a report of her trial showing how the Herald and not the chief of police had brought about the conviction. Other cases were prosecuted with the same result. The principal effort of the Herald in these cases is to satisfy the public that it is a fact that these women had carried on their business under the protection of the chief of police for many years, and to make it appear that the expose and energy of the Herald had effectually wiped out all houses of assignation.

Whereas the truth is that nothing had been accomplished except to advertise the two particular women and largely increase their business.

The three daily papers represent **THREE DISTINCT FACTIONS** in local politics. A campaign is coming on and

The Underworld Sewer

it is a question as to which paper shall have the prestige with the future officials and land its particular faction on top.

The B. faction makes terms with the monster he-landlady of the underworld, and the chief of police and the king gambler; the Herald and News factions were thus left without any influential or financial support in the lower ward for the coming campaign.

The Herald is unalterably against the chief.

The News is set against the king gambler.

The king gambler and the chief are supporters of the B. faction.

The king gambler had sued the News for libel, and obtained a verdict for several thousand dollars as damages to his reputation, because the News had published him as being implicated in a big diamond robbery; and the News was short on evidence that would stand the test of being sufficient in court.

The monster he-landlady having joined forces with the king gambler, the chief of police and the B. faction, made it necessary for the Herald and News factions to come

The One Year War

together and make a campaign for MORAL REFORM.

The victory must be won under these conditions by arousing public sentiment against the combination of the B. faction, selecting the chief of police and the two monstrosities as the special objects of attack, well knowing that the B. newspaper could not directly defend against the attacks upon the two lower ward bosses, whatever might be said against them.

It was natural under these conditions for the Herald to continue doing the chief, and the News to continue to DO the king gambler, and it was necessary for both to join hands to do the monster he-landlady of the underworld, who had not been brought before the public for some time.

The Herald and News laid the foundation to make the fight against the B. faction upon the theory that it was the natural friend of gamblers, thugs and the vicious element in general.

And in turn the B. faction charged that the H. and N. factions stood for the enforc-

The Underworld Sewer

ing of the old-fashioned blue laws, and a closed up town.

The "CRIBS" is one of the greatest money makers, considering the financial investment, which are owned by the monster helandlady, and the owner may be brought to see the error of his ways in joining the B. crowd, when it shall appear that his profits are in danger; therefore the Herald says:

> "The Cribs has been described by world travelers as the most gigantic, vicious, and degrading institutions on the entire sphere."

The following quotations indicate the nature of the information portrayed in great head lines of the News:

> "KEEP THIS IN MIND"
> "When You Vote at the Election."
> "King Gambler and His Hired Lawyer."
> WHAT ARE THEIR INTERESTS?
> The King Gambler as the leader of the gambling and criminal elements of the city, must look out for their interests in the courts. He employs his attorney for that purpose.
>
> King Gambler is used by local corporations very frequently to look after their interest when they have personal injury and other cases in court.

The One Year War

The News and Herald unite as follows:

> "The beginning, of what is declared will be a thorough investigation into the record of the Chief of Police, will be made before the board of fire and police commissioners tonight; the Health Officer will be examined as to charges that Chief of Police interfered with the board's orders. This, however, is said to be only one of numerous charges on which the board is securing evidence against the chief.

"THE CRIBS IN LIMELIGHT.

"Income of Thousands for the Owner—The He-Landlady and His Friends Interested in Promotion of the Traffic."

Chief's report with reference to houses of assignation, made to the board:

> "The chief said the houses had all been removed from the residence district and as fast as new ones came in and were discovered they were ordered removed."

For the sake of truth it is well to note that, as "fast as new ones appear" they are not removed but only ordered removed.

The Underworld Sewer

"Ministers Appeal in Police Court on Behalf of the Crib Inmates.
"HE ALLEGES DISCRIMINATION.
"The Women Are Sentenced, However, and Mayor at Once Pardons Them.

"Church Pastor Sunday Night Delivered His Address to Fire and Police Board on Social Evil.

"The Rev. Pastor Declared that Bad Women Should Be Kept in the BAD DISTRICT SET ASIDE by the City for Them.

"The Mayor Attended the Services and Tells What He Thinks About the Minister's Various Suggestions."
The judgment of the mayor is:

The One Year War

"The ministers and a great many who
listen to them do not know what they
are talking about, when they dismiss the
social evil question with the statement,
'Drive them all out of town.' Much that
the Rev. Mr. Minister said was sound,
but when he came to offering any remedy,
he, like others, fell down.

"Will driving the women out of town
really improve the situation? Or might it
not make conditions worse?

"Will not *regulated* social evil do more
for humanity than spasmodic uproars and
the throwing of a few women now and
then into cells of the city jail?"

The B. made no direct defense for the
king gambler or the monster of the underworld during the campaign.

But with their assistance managed to control the machinery of the dominant political
party.

However, the B. is careful to not recognize their influence in a public way.

After the campaign the B. presented a
lengthy editorial calculated to discredit the
motive of the other papers relating to their
attitude towards the owner of the cribs and
the social evil.

The Underworld Sewer

I quote a couple of paragraphs from the editorial as follows:

> "The resumption by certain brass band reformers of their crusade against a particular landlord in the burnt district, who seems to have disappointed them somewhere, has been seized as an occasion for a lot of hot air in their newspaper organ about the social evil."
>
> "There is no reason why these wretched fallen women should be kicked and cuffed from pillar to post and dumped into jail in the darkness of night simply to gratify some selfish purpose which has nothing to do with bettering their condition."

The editorial should say, in plain terms, if the owner of the cribs disappoints a newspaper, the women must be punished, "kicked and cuffed and dumped into jail in the darkness of the night."

In plainer terms the situation is this: The political factions seek to have the influence and money of the owner of the cribs and the king gambler, and the prestige of the chief of police.

The newspapers which are unfortunate and fail to connect with the monster of the

The One Year War

underworld and king gambler, OPEN UP a campaign against the social evil.

Thoughtful observation will show that these wars against the women of the underworld, carried on by politicians, are for the purpose of turning their money into the channel where the prosecutors of the war want it to go, or to accomplish selfish ends of some character.

If the motive should be to better the condition of unfortunate women or abolish the evil, or devise ways and means to prevent women from being driven into this horrible service, great good would come from so much energy.

In these campaigns no plans are suggested to overcome the evil, nor to better the conditions of the women; the only thought seems to be to make political capital for one side or the other and lay the foundation to be the recipient of the financial aid and personal influence of the two monsters and their subjects in the future.

The campaign was a hot one and continued after election along the skirmish lines

The Underworld Sewer

until the grand jury's report was published in the three daily journals.

The names of the grand jury disclose that they are average GOOD citizens, and must reflect the sentiment of the better element of the community.

The report came—two columns long.

For the purpose of showing what good average men regard as the proper thing to do with the social evil, after a campaign of education in the daily papers for several months, and after an exhaustive secret investigation, without regard to expense, with power to call, under oath, any citizen, male or female, within the state before their body to answer all questions that might throw light on the subject, I quote from the report a few extracts as to what should be done relating to the social evil:

> "We have made a careful investigation of conditions existing in the red light district. In our judgment a change should be made there at once.
>
> "It can certainly be controlled more effectively than is being done now."
>
> *　*　*
>
> "Another feature of the district which

The One Year War

we deem proper to condemn in the strongest terms is the practice of the large number of so-called men who infest that locality and compel these unfortunate wom-
en to furnish them money and provide
them the means with which to live."

* * *

"The worst feature of the district is
what is known as the crib system. At
night these cribs are brilliantly lighted,
the shades are never drawn, and through
the glass front or large windows therein,
that which transpires on the inside may
be observed from the street. High school
boys and boys of tender age are allowed
to visit this district and here take their
first step in vice. In our judgment this
ought not to be permitted by the authorities."

* * *

"In our judgment every place of this
character should be closed and the evil
confined as nearly as possible to houses
within the district where the shades are
always drawn and the doors closed."

* * *

"We therefore recommend that immediate steps be taken by those in authority
to close the cribs and every crib in the
city and confine the social evil to those
houses within the district where it is at
least shut out from the public view.

"We also recommend that drastic measures be resorted to for the purpose of
driving out of the city all those leprous

71

The Underworld Sewer

creatures who make a business of preying upon these women of the half world."

"Police officers, questioned by us, state that they cannot obtain the necessary evidence to convict these moral degenerates, but we of this grand jury know better. They can get the evidence, if they try."

"If they cannot get it, they should be dismissed from the force for incompetency."

* * *

"Exorbitant rents charged the women by the owners of these cribs is a menace to the city. Such a vast sum of money, derived from an illegitimate source, cannot help being a temptation to those inclined to accept bribes and graft."

* * *

"We recommend that an application be made to the next legislature that charter amendments be passed giving to such cities power to control vice in its general relation to the public therein, prescribing the district where prostitution shall be permitted to be carried on, providing for the control of inmates and those who may be there, and providing for the control of the district, so as to admit of power to prescribe the rooms and sanitation and to fix rents."

The report of the grand jury is the result of several months' agitation in the city upon

The One Year War

the social evil question, in which the news-papers have almost daily published column and double column of information.

This report stands for the highest and most intelligent thought and understanding of the people of the city.

The grand jury had authority to call, in secret, before them the newspaper reporters, the editors, the slum workers, the reformers, the ministers, the police officers, the mayor, the police judge, the gamblers, the owners of property and their agents.

They could call the women of the under-world, and their lovers, and their patrons, the keepers of houses, the collectors of rents, and in fact any citizen of the state.

After spending several weeks of investi-gation, sixteen good citizens under oath re-port their conclusions.

How can the good people of the city deny that their views are represented in this re-port?

The jury under OATH says: "We have made a careful investigation"!

The Underworld Sewer

Now mark what it is which they find to condemn:

1st. The lovers of the underworld women.

2d. The crib system.

3d. They condemn the "authorities" for allowing boys to SEE the sights through the windows.

The jury has no condemnation for the MEN who patronize and support the houses.

No condemnation for the men who start the women on the downward road.

No criticism for the men who create the conditions which result in making the social evil an institution of the civilized world.

Please do not overlook the recommendations of this representative body of men, who stand for the best element of your citizenship.

"1st. Close the cribs. 2d. CONFINE THE SOCIAL EVIL TO THE DISTRICT IN HOUSES WITH BLINDS DRAWN. 3d. Drive the lovers of the women to some other city. 4th. OBTAIN C H A R T E R AMENDMENTS GIV-

The One Year War

ING THE CITY POWER TO SET APART A PORTION OF THE CITY 'WHERE PROSTITUTION SHALL BE CARRIED ON; provide for sanitary condition; inspection,' etc.

" 'AND PROVIDING FOR THE CONTROL OF INMATES AND THOSE WHO MAY BE THERE,' 'and to fix rents.' "

GOOD PEOPLE, PLEASE DO NOT DENY THAT YOU STAND FOR THE SENTIMENT EXPRESSED IN THIS REPORT.

In short, the good people of your city propose that the city shall take charge of the women and conduct the houses and manage the business according to a well regulated and organized system, AND NOT ALLOW ANY BUT RESPECTABLE GENTLEMEN TO VISIT THE HOUSES.

The women SHALL NOT BE ALLOWED TO HAVE A RAY OF SUNSHINE OR DAYLIGHT IN THEIR ROOMS, and shall not be permitted to go

The Underworld Sewer

upon the street.   AND AT THE EX-PENSE OF THE CITY they shall be kept in a healthy condition to receive the DESIRABLE CITIZENS ONLY.

Good people, I will continue this history in order to prove THAT YOU REALLY WANT THE SOCIAL EVIL TO CON-TINUE.

If you do not want it, why do you not try to find a way to overcome it, INSTEAD OF FIGHTING A N D FUSSING OVER WHAT IS THE BEST WAY TO KEEP IT GOING?

Following the report of the grand jury one heavy editorial appeared in each of the great daily papers, in which they roasted the chief and the police board because they waited to be driven to action by the grand jury.

The B. said:

> "The report of the grand jury on the social evil has, at least, the merit of defi-niteness in pointing out the abuses that should be eradicated, although it is weak in its positive recommendations for regu-lation."

* * *

The One Year War

"There is no question but that all these features are objectionable."

* * *

"The police is to be commended for giving a month's time for the 'crib' inmates to readjust themselves rather than ordering more midnight raids, the board has shown that it is animated by a desire to correct evils rather than by the cruel frenzy of brass-band crusaders."

Can you find anything in this history that would indicate an effort to overcome the evil?

The substance of the NEWS editorial is contained in the following extracts:

"CAN YOU ANSWER? A few days ago there was running full blast a certain place that smelled to heaven in the tenderloin and is called the cribs."

* * *

"The cribs was run and is owned by a *monster* who has become wealthy from his proprietorship of the burnt district, and who has also gained fame by giving presents of money to the police department." (Do not forget, this is the News.)

"It is unfortunate that the women must be the victims of this fight instead of the monster, whose slaves they are."

"What is the board of fire and police commissioners in office for?" (This is the News, and later see the praise of this paper heaped upon this monster.)

The Underworld Sewer

Comments of News and Herald are:
"Grand Jury Stirs Public.

"Ministers Will Unite in Carrying Out Its Recommendations and Curbing the Social Evil.

"Ministerial Union Will Take Action."

Neither of the great journals ventured to suggest any method which might tend toward a reformation, or any change in the plan of treating the social evil, either for the good of the community or the reformation of the women.

"Lower Ward Cribs Closed Last Night.

"Where Will the Women Forced Out of the Cribs Go?"

This question was asked of the police commissioners and chief of police:

> Commissioner A—"Some have left town and others will try to locate in different parts of the city. Whenever it comes to the knowledge of the commissioners that they have located in the resident district they will be removed."

78

The One Year War

Commissioner B—"I can't answer that yet. It is a problem that the future will be left to solve. We will try and keep track of it very closely. If they enter the resident district they will be removed. We had hoped that they would leave town."

Commissioner C—"I do not care to discuss the question. If they move into the resident district we will take care of that when the difficulty arises."

Commissioner D—"I have no idea where they will go. They cannot go into the resident districts; that is sure."

Chief of Police—"No one can tell where they will go. Some may leave town, but not many. As to their scattering throughout the city, that is a hard proposition to forecast and we will have to handle it as best we can."

Suppose they would be good in the resident district, all the same you would throw them in jail.

Mr. Commissioner, I KNOW that you KNOW that it is in the power of your board to make it SO THAT EVERY WOMAN IN THE DISTRICT WOULD LEAVE TOWN IF YOU WERE SO DETERMINED. Nothing but jailing, and driving, and pretending to be doing something, is all you have to offer.

79

The Underworld Sewer

Head lines a few days later:

"Women Invade Residence Streets.

"Complaint Is Made to Police that Closing
of Cribs Makes Trouble."

The idea! Just as though it was something new!

> "The matter is being discussed by prominent business men and property owners, who advocate that the cribs be allowed to reopen, but that it be maintained on a stricter basis than heretofore."

This is the advice of the business men! Do not forget the business men's idea on the question.

A few months later, 1908, head lines appeared in one of the journals followed by a column of advice relating to what should be done, but not a word as to overcoming or suppressing the evil. The following is a sample of head lines:

"To Ask Reforms of Grand Jury.

"New One, Which Meets Next Monday, Will be Asked to Take Strong Measures.

The One Year War

"SOCIAL EVIL QUESTION UP.

"Reform Measures Up to New Grand
Jury."

First—"To keep disreputable women
from residence district."

Second—"Provide medical inspection of
women of ill-fame."

Third—"Regulate rents in red-light district, preventing extortion of women."

Fourth—"Drive toughs from the city."

"GRAND JURY GETS TO WORK.

"Judge ——— Delivers the Charge, Which
Refers to the Report Filed Last Week by
Chief of Police.

"Jurors Told to Ascertain Whether Recommendations of Last Grand Jury Are Carried out."

"GRAND JURY KEEPS ON PROBING.

"It Will See if Public Officials Carried Out
Recommendations of Last Jury.

81

The Underworld Sewer

"Judge Gives Instructions.

"GOOD MEN ON THE JURY."

Let us now test public sentiment by the instructions of the high court to the grand jury, from which I quote a few extracts. The court said:

> "Gentlemen of the Grand Jury: You have been called at this time for the purpose of subserving the betterment of good government in Blank county. The institutions of a people are not, and will not be, anything over and beyond what the people demand. The only inquisition for and on behalf of the people wherein they can have investigated and declared the status of their law enforcement is the grand jury, unless legislative inquiry be instituted."
>
> * * *
>
> "Generally speaking, conditions will be what the people demand, and the law will be administered according to the requirements of the people. So we need not find fault with the past; so we must address ourselves to the future. I take it for granted that the report of the last grand jury, in which all joined, declared conditions as then known. That being true, nothing could be so seemly and proper as another grand jury to find out whether or not those conditions have improved."

The One Year War

"If there are men who live by pimpage,
that is, off the earnings of fallen women,
they hanging around for that purpose and
so living, it is your duty to indict them."

The instructions of the court to the grand
jury are a matter of record and are lengthy,
as well as the report of the jury. It may be
said that the grand jury may not reflect the
sentiment of the good people, notwithstanding these are good men. But when the judge
of the high court expresses opinions publicly, it surely is expected to be about the best
that can be offered on moral questions.

If the reader does not already believe that
the good people of the land, by their acts and
conduct, encourage, foster and maintain the
social evil and would not have it abolished,
THIS TRUE HISTORY WILL CER-
TAINLY PROVE that such is the la-
mentable and unconscious fact.

There is not one sentence in the instruction of the court which indicates that there
is any desire to suppress or overcome the
evil, or to devise or recommend ways and
means to make it possible to stop the continual supply of women to the underworld.

83

The Underworld Sewer

Now while the grand jury is in session bringing witnesses of all kinds and character, relating to the social evil and, it is known that a part of the program is to present an indictment of some kind against the owner of the cribs, it must be observed that it is true to history that every time a man of that character makes terms with a newspaper, he does something which gives that paper an excuse to sound his praise.

The NEWS is the paper which had most prominently held the crib owner up before the public, painted in the most horrid colors; this is the newspaper which had published him as the most wicked character in the universe, and HAD KEPT HIM BEFORE THE PEOPLE AS THE MOST MERCILESS VAMPIRE THAT EVER DREW BREATH.

This he-landlady of the scum of the underworld sought out a poor old man, having a crippled and sickly daughter, each of which have but a few years at most to live.

This old father and his dying child were in destitute circumstances, just the same as

The One Year War

hundreds and hundreds of other old men and their sick daughters, now in the city, and have been for years.

THIS MURDEROUS SLAVE DRIVER OF HUNDREDS AND HUNDREDS OF FALLEN WOMEN SUDDENLY BECAME A PUBLIC BENEFACTOR, AND THIS PARTICULAR NEWSPAPER SOUNDED HIS PRAISE TO THE SKY, as though he was the first man in the city who had relieved a poor and sick person.

I refer to this in disgust, because I am forced to recognize the fact that this sudden change of front on the part of this newspaper toward the he-landlady is a queer move, but not unusual.

The following are some of the great head lines at different times:

"FORMER CRIB OWNER ANNOUNCES HE WILL MOVE INVALIDS INTO NEW HOMES."

"HE WILL PAY THEIR RENT."

"FURTHER DECLARES HE WILL ALSO PROVIDE FOR THEIR FUTURE WELFARE."

The Underworld Sewer

"Cottage Is Secured."

"A cottage has been rented for the poor family at Blank street and the family is moving in this afternoon. The cottage is high and dry and is expected to be very comfortable and in a healthy location."

Which lines are followed by a column of praise for the crib owner, giving details as to the present life of the father, who is 75 years old, and "poor little May with her new crutches presented to her by the crib owner."

I am tempted to quote at least half a column of this write-up just to show how a newspaper can fill its columns with sensational gush with the hope of obtaining the good will of a grand jury toward such a criminal.

This crib owner, and "benefactor" who OWNS ROWS OF BIG HOUSES IN THE RED-LIGHT DISTRICT WHERE THE "BLINDS ARE ALWAYS DRAWN AND THE DOORS CLOSED" AND WHOSE INCOME IS $75,000 A YEAR, WHO HAS FOR THE FIRST TIME IN HIS LIFE DONE A CHARITABLE ACT, and has

The One Year War

publicly pledged his honor to "CARE FOR
A WHOLE FAMILY AS LONG AS
ANY OF THEM SHALL LIVE," is for
many weeks daily praised in columns of this
newspaper, WHICH SO THOROUGH-
LY DENOUNCED HIM A FEW
MONTHS AGO.

Here are some more head lines, followed
by much praise for the "benefactor":

"LITTLE MAY HAS TRAINED NURSE.

"Takes Suddenly Worse Saturday and
Benefactor Comes to Her Aid."

"The best of medical attention is being
given the child and hopes are now entertained that the change in atmosphere and
the hand of plenty will save her life."

(A day or two later.)

"MAY TO GO TO SUNDAY SCHOOL.

"Benefactor Buys New Dress."

If you and the grand jury are not satisfied
that the crib owner has changed some
SPOTS and made amends for all the misery
and degradation he has brought upon his

The Underworld Sewer

slaves in the underworld, and that he is now truly a benefactor, please see the Daily News; there is an elaborate picture covering the front page of this influential newspaper, the old father and the daughter, also the old house and the new house, an old picture and a new one of the benefactor, and if you are then not satisfied that the slave owner has not exchanged some of his thousands for glory, look up the files of this paper and read its many columns.

The newspaper creates public sentiment; it is the most powerful lever for good or evil; without its influence no great reformation can be accomplished in this age.

Unless positively demonstrated, one could not believe that a daily newspaper would for any consideration so suddenly and radically change from the merited condemnation to the unmerited and uncalled for praise of such character of man as this.

Although this praise did not have the effect to prevent the indictment by the grand jury, it had a soothing-syrup effect upon the public.

The One Year War

That which this slave driver did is commendable. But the charitable men and women often do as much, which is paragraphed in ten lines, if it is referred to at all.

I bring this incident into this history because it shows the great influence which a he-landlady has power to swing in a city.

This indictment will probably remain on the program for a year or two, and that will be the end of it; or a small fine may be imposed, but the monster has been thoroughly advertised as A WEALTHY REAL ESTATE MAN AND A PUBLIC BENEFACTOR.

Little May died just twenty-two days after she was adopted by the slave driver. (This was the WHOLE LIFE of little May.)

It is now several months since the old grand jury reported, and the campaign of education upon the social evil has continued.

The official record of the police department shows that there is no social evil in the resident district; that the cribs are all closed; that the city is rid of all hangers-on around

The Underworld Sewer

the red-light district, and the social evil is under good control of the police department; the new grand jury is called and instructed by the court as though the records of the police department are a snare and a delusion, if not absolutely false.

The new grand jury, fresh from the people, consisting largely of eminent citizens, and representing the better element, including the churches, has made extended investigations and make their report. I prove by this history that there IS NO PUBLIC SENTIMENT EXISTING AGAINST THE CONTINUATION OF THE EVIL in this country, but, on the contrary, the highest and prevalent public sentiment is that the social evil should be legalized and controlled by the city or other authority; that the women should have official medical examination and be kept free from disease, for the safety of the men who patronize them.

I will quote from the report of the last grand jury, June 1, 1908, for final and conclusive proofs of the truth of my statement.

The One Year War

The jury recommends as follows:

"1st. That the cribs system be abolished.

"2nd. That the *police commissioners appoint a physician to examine those women* and issue to them proper *certificates*.

"3rd. *We deem it necessary to tolerate such conditions*, but insist that the fire and police commissioners compel the removal of such houses from the resident districts.

"4th. It (the social evil) has been openly promoted and advertised by some of our citizens in a large district in the eastern portion of our city; it is also found to a greater extent than ever before in the residence district, and no part of the city can feel that it is free or safe from this vice, as at present handled by our police officials."

This grand jury further says it is now worse than ever, notwithstanding the report of the police department to the contrary.

The grand jury further reports as follows:

"5th. But from the evidence submitted there still remains a large number of these 'human vampires' as a menace to morality and good government.

"We believe that these women should be compelled by ordinance or legislation to keep off the streets and not allowed to exhibit themselves at or solicit from the windows."

The Underworld Sewer

It does seem as though there should be some method by which the women of the underworld might be allowed an occasional ray of daylight and sunshine, or at least a breath of pure air.

Will the good men stop to consider what they would do if shut in as they advise, relating to these women, with starvation at hand?

Do you call such treatment humane or sanitary?

The "human vampires" refers to the lovers of the women of the underworld.

True to nature, if there is anything on earth that the gentlemen who patronize the underworld hate, it is the lovers of the women. These gentlemen who patronize and support the public house are, in fact, jealous of these "vampires" who hold the love of the women of the underworld.

Mr. Juror, the women of the underworld do not solicit the companionship and association of their customers for any attraction they have for us, outside of the financial question, as a rule the women despise their

The One Year War

customers, how could it be otherwise. The women regard it as the worst of hardships to entertain the customer and only tolerate and endure the suffering of their company for the purpose of obtaining that miserable piece of money.

The customer goes into their district for the purpose of spending his money to good advantage; the more starved these girls are, the cheaper can they be bought into slavery, yet YOU, MR. JUROR, CAN CONCEIVE OF NO BETTER WAY THAN TO SEND THEM TO JAIL IF THEY SHOW THEIR FACES.

> The jury said: "Further, we recommend that if the owners of these houses are charging exorbitant rents, that it shall be reported to the proper authorities, where an adjustment can be made satisfactory to all concerned."

This would be very kind to the women, for the city to protect them from exorbitant rents.

However, this would not help them so much as these kind hearted persons think, because these same patrons would expect to

The Underworld Sewer

buy a slave still cheaper on the strength of the reduction; in any event, THE PA-TRON, THE POLICE, THE LOVER, THE LANDLORD, USURP THE MONEY OF THE UNDERWORLD.

These reports of the grand jury show that all this agitation leaves the city in the SAME CONDITION AS IT WAS WHEN THE WAR STARTED.

The following is an extract from one of the papers upon this point:

> "The general opinion that assignation houses exist in all parts of our city has been materially strengthened by testimony before this body, and we believe that the police department is largely responsible for this."

Editorial comments:

> "The indictment of a few specially selected offenders in the social evil business may serve as object lessons or scapegoats, but it is manifest that every one of these cases could just as easily have been prosecuted through the county attorney's office."
>
> * * *
>
> "As to the recommendations of the grand jury embodied in the dual report,

The One Year War

for the most part they simply endorse
and approve the policies already put into
effect by the present police board, although the one recommendation in the nature of a new departure, namely, that of
official medical certification of women of
the town, presents a very doubtful proposition."

Editorial:

"Some months ago there was a strong
public sentiment aroused in this city
against the presence of assignation houses
and houses of prostitution in the residence
section of our city.

"This sentiment became so strong that
the board of fire and police commissioners were forced to take some action, and,
consequently, they instructed the chief of
police to close all such houses.

"The chief of police, some time later,
returned a report to the board of fire and
police commissioners to the effect that *he
had closed all such houses* in the residence
district and that *none longer existed*.

"This report was absolutely false, a fact
known to a great number of our citizens
and whose falsity could have been easily
verified by the members of the board of
fire and police commissioners.

"By their acceptance and approval of
this false report of the chief of police, the
members of the board were as much responsible for this lie as he."

The Underworld Sewer

Editorial:

> "The appointment of a physician to ex-
> amine women of the district is urged. The
> abolishment of the social evil in the res-
> idence district is demanded and a recom-
> mendation made that if it continues, re-
> sponsible officers be removed from office.
> The police department is urged to cleanse
> the city of those men who live off of the
> earnings of women of the town."

No one makes any claim that the conditions relating to the evil is really bettered by
the work and the expenses of two grand juries, amounting to many thousands of dollars.

The public mind is settled down to the
belief that the only thing that can be done
for the betterment of conditions, is more
stringent rules and regulations that will re-
strict the public houses to a certain part of
the city, keep it sanitary, prohibit the women
from appearance on the street, keep them in
dark rooms, and require them to be examined
by physicians, for THE SAFETY OF
THE GENTLEMEN WHO PAT-
RONIZE THEM. Even to go further,
protect them from extortionate rent, and
from the men, not only who pay them no

The One Year War

money, but who by acting the part of a lover are assisted by the women.

In other words, DRIVE OUT OF TOWN ALL MEN WHO ARE DEAD BEATS in the underworld, or DO NOT PAY MONEY FOR THE SUPPORT OF THE INSTITUTION.

Within one year the third grand jury, after two months' work, make a report which is published in the daily press.

The report severely censures the mayor and police department. The following is an extract:

> "We regret to report that we do not find conditions with reference to prostitution improved in the down-town district, outside of the so-called red-light district.
>
> "We are convinced that there has been an improvement in the red-light district during the past year."

The improvements in the cribs (heretofore described) ARE THAT A SECOND STORY HAS BEEN ADDED. THE CRIBS WERE ONE STORY IN THE BEGINNING OF THE YEAR, NOW THEY ARE TWO STORY HOUSES. No one can deny that this is an improvement.

The Underworld Sewer

These places are now capable of accommodating twice as many girls and of yielding more than double profit for the owners.

We hope this is not the improvement, referred to by the grand jury, although THERE IS NO OTHER VISIBLE TO THE NAKED EYE AT PRESENT.

An editorial said:

> "The grand jury, which so scathingly criticised our city officials for neglect of duty, did not seem to have the courage of its convictions sufficient to bring indictments."
>
> "This is true, even though it uncovers no new conditions of affairs, but practically reiterated what two previous grand juries have said."

The stand I am taking is that if the people so desired the underworld evil could be wiped out. This is supported by the following extract from its report: "The mayor and Board of Police Commissioners are clothed with legal power and authority to control or stop prostitution."

The fact still remains that the people will not put men in control of city, state and national government, who would DARE pro-

The One Year War

hibit the social evil. ALL OF WHICH
PROVES THAT THE PEOPLE
WANT THE INSTITUTION.

This chapter is true to history and has
been written within the year, as events oc-
curred. They are no new statements. You
will recognize them as having heard them
all your life, WHICH A BLUSH
SHOULD ACCOMPANY THAT
WOULD NOT RUB OFF.

The purpose of publishing this history
will be largely accomplished if good men
and women will open their eyes to the awful
facts that they are deceived and misled into
the idea that when they give such methods
their approval, WITHOUT ATTEMPT-
ING TO REMEDY THE FOUNDA-
TION OF THE EVIL, they are simply
FOSTERING, PROTECTING, EN-
COURAGING AND MAINTAINING
the social evil.

CHAPTER VI.

Man the Aggressor

Man robs woman of her purity under a pretense that he is interested in her affairs, and will protect her in her good name and reputation and **THAT HE NEVER WILL DESERT HER.**

Man robs woman of her purity by pretense of affection and **UNFATHOMABLE LOVE.**

Man robs woman of her purity by marrying her and driving her out into the world; and by **NOT SUPPLYING HER WITH MONEY** to furnish the necessities of life.

Man robs woman of her purity by **LEADING HER ON WITH PRESENTS AND FAVORS.**

100

"ON THE DOWNWARD ROAD"

Man the Aggressor

Man robs woman of her purity as a RE-WARD FOR HAVING BEFRIEND-ED HER.

Man robs woman of her purity by leading her into apparently innocent but question-able paths, under PRETENSE OF PLEASANT SOCIETY.

Who is the greater robber, the person who steals my money or the one who steals my reputation, my character, my soul?

> "He who filches from me my purse steals *trash;* but he who takes from me my good name steals that which does not *enrich him* but makes *me poor* in-deed."

Men who start women on the downward road can be found in all classes. Some men who lead women to ruin BOAST ABOUT IT, tell their men friends how it was accom-plished, and REGARD IT AS A HUGE JOKE. Other men who have been guilty of the same crime are very reticent on the sub-ject and are ever ready to deny it and will even commit perjury in so doing if neces-sary.

A girl is never too humble or too helpless

The Underworld Sewer

for a man to desecrate. A girl's refinement and education does not always protect her against man's low nature. They are told that this thing has ALWAYS EXISTED and ALWAYS WILL exist; to attempt an explanation to the contrary is met with DIREFUL CONTEMPT AND DERISION.

Where is the man that will not do the best he knows how to PREVENT HIS OWN daughter, wife or sister from such a fate although at the same time he may be degraded, and among the vilest of vile.

Again, a young man may appear well in society and be respectable in reputation but will work all kinds of schemes to involve the reputation of the sister of some other man, yet he will be one that would defend his own sister against insults and protect her in all ways.

Although a man will, under conditions of safety and secrecy, take advantage of a beautiful, innocent, modest, lovely young woman who is the daughter, sister or wife of some other man, YET HE WOULD ADVISE

Man the Aggressor

HER TO TRUST NO OTHER MAN in such a way.

If such an opportunity presents itself and the man does not take advantage of his chance, for this surrender he thinks he deserves notice, and tells his friends about it, but he is ridiculed, dubbed a CHUMP, or designated as an ANGEL TOO GOOD FOR THIS WORLD. Such is the undeveloped morality of the modern young man.

It is woman's nature to look upon her companion as a protector with no thought of guile. A man does not tell his victim that he is only sowing his wild oats, that he is not ready to marry and settle down. And when he and society deserts her and she descends step by step to the underworld her fate does not seem to concern anybody; until some blubbering reformer comes to redeem her from the sewer.

Not so with the destroyer. He remains up there in society and has not lost his standing in the business world. True, there was some gossip about him and a girl at one time but the girl has disappeared now! If the

The Underworld Sewer

man had been guilty of some other misdemeanor society would have snubbed him, but not for getting a girl talked about. SOCIETY ALWAYS BLAMES A GIRL FOR GETTING TALKED ABOUT. This gossip is the first step downward. The man is the aggressor, and the Christian world is an accomplice.

Because men have never been taught TO CURB THEIR DESIRES is the PRODUCING CAUSE of the MOST BRUTAL CONDITIONS KNOWN TO MANKIND. It blasts the happiness of thousands of families in our nation every year, and GOOD PEOPLE, FAILING TO COMPREHEND THE CAUSE, DISMISS IT, or ATTRIBUTE IT TO ANY CAUSE EXCEPT THE RIGHT ONE, and even claim that a woman is first to invite her own downfall. THIS CLAIM IS THE MOST DECEPTIVE LIE THAT WAS EVER UTTERED. Every woman who has fallen knows it is a lie and men who have been the cause know it is a lie.

Man the Aggressor

Since Eve was on earth (and she was first tempted by a serpent) A GIRL OR WOMAN NEVER LIVED WHO WAS BOLD ENOUGH TO MAKE THE FIRST ADVANCE TO A MAN.

This same serpent can be found everywhere today ready to destroy souls. In modern times the serpent is in human form, AND IS GENERALLY KNOWN AS A MAN.

It is an old story that Eve tempted Adam. It is also conceded that ADAM WAS AN "ALL-AROUND LIAR" and the FATHER OF LIES.

105

CHAPTER VII.

Our Society

There are many classes of society in the underworld. Our best society is made up of the beautiful, well-educated, witty, fascinating and refined women who have been teachers in schools and in private homes. Also those who have had experience in business offices as confidential clerks and stenographers. Also those from the counter of the large fashionable stores. And young wives who have been abandoned by their husbands, leaving them without money or ability to support themselves and their children.

This class of women are entertainers. They retain their modesty better than those who are not educated and those not accustomed to the ideas of men of business and society. These are more attractive to men of means who are not seeking the lower and more vulgar side of the underworld. There are pub-

Our Society

lic houses in large cities which are kept supplied with this class of women and will take no other. Beauty, either natural or artificial, enhances men's admiration of women in OUR society as well as in that of the Christian world.

This class of women who constitute OUR HIGHEST society in the underworld, are as far removed from those occupying cheap dives and cribs as are the millionaire's daughters from the girls born and raised in rag-cat alley. While the millionaire's daughter will never reach the condition existing in rag-cat alley the woman of our highest society in the underworld comes to the lowest dive and crib as certain as time goes on unless she dies or quits the business.

By what road does this high class of our women reach the underworld? By two broad ways, men's double-dealing, deception and lust; and by deprivation, poverty and abuse. Here is one example which holds good in hundreds of cases.

A teacher who is supporting her mother and educating her younger sisters, works

The Underworld Sewer

hard and conscientious in her school. She becomes acquainted with a young man who is also a stranger in the community. He escorts her everywhere. They are engaged to be married. On account of his gallantry and generosity she becomes deeply involved in the love which absorbs self control and discretion, which the desecrater has not failed to observe. He is aware of his wonderful power over his victim. Where he leads she follows; to every overture she acquiesces. They are soon to be united in marriage, he tells her. Time goes on. They are seen much together in compromising places. But the young school teacher realizes only one fact, which is that she is soon to wed the man she loves.

There are whisperings about her in the neighborhood and later on a scandal. The young man disappears. The truth has become known—the young man was a married man with a family in an adjoining state. The girl is broken hearted. She cannot go home and bring disgrace upon her mother and sisters. Her grief she cannot tell to

Our Society

any one. The secrets of her shame she must hide. Suicide suggests itself to her, but she dismisses it as an intrusion and applies for aid and finds it in the home of the Salvation Army.

She remains for some time. When she emerges there is a mite of humanity left behind for adoption who is wholly unaware of the disgrace hanging over him. He is as innocent and pure as any other babe. Among the strange things that will be explained within the next step of enlightenment will be why an individual should be held to answer for a sin for which he is not responsible. Any inherited tendency can be removed by the proper appliance but it is the stigma with which civilization stamps it that cannot be removed.

This sad and lonely girl comes to the underworld. This reserved, frightened beauty becomes the "belle of the ball." She is observed by the wealthy patrons of the gilded palace as one who knows nothing of the underworld and the more she shies and shrinks from the approach of the gentlemen from

The Underworld Sewer

the Christian world the more eagerly she is sought by them.

I am not writing of a myth, but of facts which have come under my observation.

Among her customers is the rich society gentleman who is noted in his "set" for his eccentricities. The truth is he is addicted to the habit of opium smoking and in the underworld is known as a hop-fiend.

He takes the girl to apartments furnished for the occasion, which is being presided over by a Chinaman dressed in white linen. There is a reclining chair made for two. A little table is cut in the wood in the lower part of the arm between the double chair. There the big bowl of the hop-pipe rests, the stem of which is long enough to use without bending the head. The mouthpiece of the stem is nearly seven inches in circumference, over which the smoker stretches his mouth, and then one long inhalation and the stem is passed to the companion, who follows suit. It is handed back and forth until the pipe is empty.

The size of the outside of the pipe is as big

Our Society

as two fists but it must not be supposed that it has a large opening like a pipe. The bowl which holds the opium is about a quarter of an inch in diameter. On the little table is a very small lamp that has a small streak of light over which the opium is "cooked." Over this blaze the opium is held on a long bladed knife until it is hot. Then it is laid on the side of the pipe and worked very much as bread is kneaded—then held over the blaze again and again and kneaded until the right shade of color is reached.

To remove some of the poison, opium must go through this process before it is fit to smoke.

The amount of opium used for each pipe is about the size of a pea and it costs about three dollars each time the pipe is refilled. For those who have "lay-outs" at home, a jar containing five ounces of hop may be purchased for eight dollars.

One who uses opium for the first time resolves never to do so again. The result is a deathly sickness. But he is curious to know how it will affect him the next time and thus

111

The Underworld Sewer

it is tried again and again. At first it is intended as an experiment only but the outcome is the hop-fiend.

This hop-joint becomes the rendezvous for the society dude and the belle of the underworld. She found that she did not worry so much about her mother and sisters, to whom she seldom wrote. She becomes stupefied with opium and cares less and less for her surroundings. Two years elapsed and she was no longer the belle of the underworld—other girls had taken her place. Another year passes and—behold a wreck. She has parted with her belongings and even her clothing for opium, and would now beg, borrow or steal the money to obtain the drug. She has no regrets, no hope, no longings, no desire for anything but opium. This is the end of a beautiful and wretched human being, at the mercy of conditions of today.

The dope and cigarette habits are simply appalling among us—more than half of the underworld girls use morphine, cocaine, or hop in some form or other. On account of the lax drug laws there is no restrictions

Our Society

upon them. They are able to buy as much as they want and the amount consumed can scarcely be equaled by the smart set. It would almost seem that the doctors and druggists are in league to make as many fiends as possible for the benefit of their business. But it isn't wholly the doctor's fault. The girls learn it from each other and from their lovers.

The statement that the madams of the underworld are responsible for girls' dope habits is erroneous. They try to keep it from them and have stringent rules for that purpose. Only one who is a dope fiend herself will try to get some one to join her, as fiends, like misery, love company.

—

Most of the girls learn to smoke cigarettes as soon as they enter the underworld. Most men smoke and with the help of the women the house becomes so dense that one who does not smoke cannot endure it. Those who have conquered the cigarette habit or attempted to do so know that it is not the easiest thing in the world. But it becomes less difficult for

The Underworld Sewer

the fiend to break it up if he can fix upon a time in the future when he may return to the cigarette. He knows it is a false bait, but it induces determination to reach the point of his resolution, meantime the craving for them diminishes—in the beginning the fiend would rather be dead than to think that he would never, NEVER, have another cigarette.

I am well acquainted with a woman who had used them incessantly for more than twenty years. July 22, 1906, she decided to abstain from cigarette smoking for THIRTY YEARS. This was done in the midst of smoke which is said to be dense enough to cut with a knife in which she remained until the following year—this was to test her perseverance.

Leaving the underworld had been in her mind for several years. She realized that she must correct her habits and that it must be done right there in the thickest of temptation. This was the penance by which she was to earn respect and confidence in herself.

The proper motive will enable one to aban-

Our Society

don any habit. Cigarette smoking deadens the faculties and weakens the will power, not to mention the injurious effect it has upon the health. Think of the absurdity of pumping smoke into the lungs where nature has made no plans except for pure air.

By her experience this woman is convinced that all fiends can cut out the cigarette if they have a proper motive inducing their determination.

To protect the weak young man and woman who burn up their energy there should be laws made and enforced to prohibit the cigarette. Some states have legislated that way but the laws have been a dead letter.

CHAPTER VIII.

A Cause

Miss Douglass was educated at one of the colleges in a neighboring city. She was also recognized as the most accomplished girl in the village. Her father was the sole proprietor of a large country store. The financial crisis of 1893 swept away his fortune and in the struggle to overcome the tide his health as well as his mind gave away, and to make a complete wreck—according to the old saying that misfortune never comes single—he was thrown from a vehicle by a runaway horse and crippled for life. It then became obvious that Miss Douglass was the only support of her invalid parents, her mother having been hopelessly afflicted with ill health for years and this made it necessary for Miss Douglass to put her education to use by giving music lessons.

Under such conditions it would not be an

A Cause

unusual occurrence that she should have the sympathy of her father's friends and her own acquaintances in her distress and poverty, struggling at her music teaching from house to house and working at home to make ends meet. One after another of her father's acquaintances tendered her their good will. She had the love and respect of the whole community.

For several years she labored without any change in her condition. She was beautiful and the picture of health and would have had any number of offers of marriage, but as fate would have it she had her parents to care for, whom she always called her "children." There was no young man brave enough to assume the responsibility of marrying Miss Douglass and her children.

The leading politician and also the wealthiest man in the village had often insisted upon loaning her money which she declined except in extreme cases of necessity. He was a married man whose wife had gone east to visit her parents, accompanied by the two children, but had failed to return. This

The Underworld Sewer

happened three years before. The wife had in the meantime applied for and had been granted separate maintenance. This man became more and more bold and would way-lay Miss Douglass in every possible manner, just to talk a few moments. These intrusions made her life most miserable. MISS DOUGLASS WAS A GOOD GIRL WHOSE THOUGHTS WERE OF HER CHILDREN ONLY. Yet he continually attracted her attention. For months and months he would put himself in her way and make proposals to which she would not listen.

One day she was called to an adjoining city to give a lesson. Here he also followed with urging and offering of money, assuring her that she could never pay the doctor, the butcher, the baker, by means of giving music lessons. She thought of the bills that were piling up, the unpaid house rent, and of the many necessities she could furnish her sick parents. Under stress of such circumstances and the most positive and certain caution and conditions of secrecy she yields

A Cause

to his demand, which calls for only an occasional visit to a most private assignation house.

It was not a great while until there was an uproar of scandal which plunged the girl into hysterical weeping, who realized too late that she had been enticed and had fallen into an awful self-sacrifice, and as usual must receive the greater blame. The opportunity for a display of Christian charity was at hand, but no aid came to save this forsaken girl. Merely expressions of censure and disdain were heard everywhere.

Miss Douglass, who had committed this unpardonable sin, was not a coward. She remained with her sick parents—"her children"—until the last, which happened within a short time.

Miss Douglass became a member of a dramatic company for a while and later to furnish music for a dance hall, from there to join the fashionable underworld society.

This sounds like fiction, but it is a true abbreviated history of a beautiful girl in the underworld.

The Underworld Sewer

One day I overheard a conversation between Miss Douglass and another girl. The girl said:

"You have been here just three months today, Douglass."

"Have I? Well, it seems to me a lifetime."

"This is a cruel and unrelenting world in which we live. My experience compels me sometime to believe that there are no good people in it. Yet I know it isn't the world, but the people who have taken possession of it who are to blame. The earth was donated by the Creator to the human race, not to a preferred class, but to all of his people. But the strongest and best fed branch of the human race have not only gobbled up the land but also the resources of the earth. More than half of the human family are only tenants and have no more right to the earth than they have to the planets above. Go where you will and you must pay some one to live there. Those who are unable to pay have the choice of alternatives—either to get off the earth, or get the money to pay the rent, whether by fair or foul means—mil-

A Cause

lions of women must resort to the foulest
of all means to obtain the money to pay some
one for the privilege of living on the earth."

"Are we supposed to be reconciled and
satisfied with our fate down here?"

"Supposed to, by whom?" inquired the
girl.

"By those who are called good people, of
course," replied Douglass.

"Did you ever have any thoughts of us before you came here?"

"No; but then I was just a lone girl,
and had other things to think about. Besides,
I didn't know, except in a vague way, that
such places existed."

"To the best of my knowledge," said the
girl, "WE ARE THE LEAST OF THE
GOOD PEOPLE'S TROUBLE. Why
should we be? Look at the vast benefit we
are to every town in so many different ways.
Take this building, for instance. It rents
for $400 a month. The owner is a rich man
and very influential. I know him. I used
to work for his wife at one time trimming
hats for the children, and doing sewing. He
has a nice family."

The Underworld Sewer

"Well, why are you not there now instead of where you are?"

"Now Douglass, you know that no one comes here without a cause. I will tell you some day. I will say this much now—that a man who is employed in his office put me here."

"Does the proprietor of this house come here?" inquired Douglass.

"Not that anybody knows about. We are not supposed to know all that goes on about this house. You have noticed haven't you, that when the door bell rings all of us girls rush to the stairs and 'rubber'? Well, occasionally all the electric lights will suddenly be turned out in the corridor below."

"I have observed once or twice such an occurrence, but could not account for the cause of it."

"Well, we have formed our inference as to the cause of it and that is all that is necessary here. But it does not concern us. Douglass, you see that big house just across the street? No, not that row, nor that line over there. All that and a lot more belongs to

A Cause

a notorious thing which everybody knows. I mean the large one to the left with the swell front. That house rents for $500 a month. The owner would not have it known to his church friends that he has property down here for the world."

"Do you mean to tell me that we earn the money which buys the dresses to go to church in?"

"It amounts to about that. Douglass, when you have been here three months longer you will know some of the reasons why the good people do not worry about us."

"What about the cribs of which I heard so much talk a year ago? Are they all gone?" inquired Douglass.

"Yes. They are all gone—GONE UP ONE STORY HIGHER, like mushrooms in a single night."

"But what was the cause of the sudden growth?"

"The cause of it," said the girl, "was to comply with the command of the grand juries, that girls must live in houses with 'blinds drawn' instead of cribs. This district

123

The Underworld Sewer

we are in is really an institution. The property of course belongs to individuals and corporations, but the INSTITUTION BELONGS TO THE CITY. Changes and improvements are made here by the city according to requirements."

"The newspaper agitation against this district—" inquired Douglass. "Is it always a bluff?"

"Yes, always; it don't mean anything at all, at least not what it pretends to mean. I will tell you more about it tomorrow; there goes the dinner gong—let us go down."

"But 'isn't it awful, Mabel,' this condition you have told me about; that this district should be maintained as a 'catch all' for those who have committed, by force of circumstances, the unpardonable sin?"

"That," said Mabel, "is true. But the sin is made lawful here for those who remain in the district; IT IS LAWFUL," she repeated; "don't misunderstand me."

"I see," said the other. "I think I will reform."

"Why, Douglass, you would stand no

A Cause

more show than a snow-ball in—you know where. I have tried it."

"Then we must be consigned to the sulphurous fumes of the underworld and be eternally damned here and hereafter; is that what you mean?"

"Now you are talking, Douglass. I hate to tell you, but such are the facts. No one stops to consider whether it is worth while to bring about a condition that would free us from such a life."

"Well, I know what I can——"

"Hush, Douglass; don't say it, forget it, dear," she said softly. "Come; they are not very friendly down stairs if we chance to be late for dinner."

Douglass hesitated a moment, and then said: "Oh! let the dinner go. We may not have another opportunity to talk, and now while there is no one present to interrupt us, tell me the meaning of 'white slave traffic.' Mabel, can you explain it?"

"Well, it refers to"—and she let out a string of oaths that piled upon each other like the roaring of thunder, winding up

125

The Underworld Sewer

with a crash. She sprang to her feet, and walked the floor back and forth, and then grabbed a newspaper from a rack on the wall, scanning its columns.

"My! how you swear!" You frighten me!" said Douglass. "When you get your breath, will you answer my question?"

"The condition which beset womankind from every direction," said Mabel—her eyes flashed—"is enough to make a saint swear. It is the only way to express our opinion of things, or abhorrence of them down here. Read this paragraph; it will furnish some of the information you want," pointing to a column. Douglass took the paper and slowly read:

> "The white slave traffic is a system—a syndicate which has its ramifications from the Atlantic seaboard to the Pacific ocean, with 'clearing houses' or 'distributing centers' in nearly all of the larger cities; that in this ghastly traffic the buying price of a young girl is $15 and that the selling price is generally about $200—if the girl is especially attractive the white slave dealer may be able to sell her for $400 or $600; that this syndicate did not make less than $200,000 last year in this almost

126

A Cause

unthinkable commerce; that it is a defi-
nate organization, sending its hunters regularly to scour France, Germany, Hun-
gary, Italy and Canada for victims; that
the man at the head of this unthinkable
enterprise is known among his hunters as
'The Big Chief.'"

"I don't blame you for swearing, Mabel;
this reveals a shocking condition, but no
more so than our own," she said in a choked
voice. "I see this paragraph is from Edwin
W. Sims' investigations, 'Why Girls Go
Astray,' and that the book may be obtained
at the Currier Publishing Company, Chi-
cago. I shall send for it."

"The condition," said Mabel, "is a branch
of brutality, from the same economic roots
existing in every state in the union, which
makes it possible for victims of poverty to
be lured into this slavery by countless num-
bers every year."

At this period a colored maid had pushed
her way into the room; she said: "I was
sent up here to see why you all don't come to
dinner." To which no one made a reply.
Mabel stepped into her own room and
brought back some money. And Douglass
rummaged in a drawer for the same reason.

127

The Underworld Sewer

On the way down stairs we met a bunch of girls; some were smoking cigarettes, and some were rolling them. One of them said to us: "You will catch it." Each of us was busy with her own thoughts, and kept silent. Arriving in the dining room, which we found deserted, except for an attendant, to whom the girls gave liberal tips, and also sent fees to the cook. In a few minutes the dinner was served hot. Not a word was uttered during the meal. These two stately beauties, whose thoughts were so far above their condition, left the dining room in silence.

The gilded palace is worse than the dive of the vilest; the latter represents the true condition, while the palace gives to vice a dangerous polish which hides some of its ghastliness.

The girls you meet in the hallways, in the parlors, everywhere, are of different types of beauty, but a close observer will behold the stamp upon their different features of bewilderment, fear, unutterable sadness, resignation, dread, defiance and despair. The wonder is how a system can exist so calloused as to consign them to such a life.

CHAPTER IX.

Betrayal

Betrayal under the promise or **marriage** is one of the most common causes which drives the girl away from her home and friends and eventually precipitates her into the depth of poverty and thrusts her into the underworld, because the way there is made so easy.

The following is a briefly told experience of a young girl who has just awakened from dreamland to a realization that she is obliged to choose between suicide or escape from the vicinity of her sorrow and disgrace.

But for the baneful influence of the WOLF who beguiled and dazzled her by wild romances to take the wrong step, the girl would have remained pure and good, as would many thousands of others, now in the underworld.

With no knowledge of the world and its

The Underworld Sewer

wickedness she drifts on, to seek a position in an office, in a store, in a factory, or as a domestic; her money is exhausted; there is no refuge provided where she would be welcome and no questions asked; she is in no humor to give an account of herself, death would be far easier—it is an old story, and because this story is so old, convinces us that all that is rotten does not lay in Denmark.

Wherever she applied for work she was requested to furnish reference, which she could not do. She had only her besmirched reputation at home, where her betrayer still remains in society; she must conceal her identity, and by so doing is regarded with suspicion.

She finds no employment, she is hungry, but she observes an abundance of food everywhere, hotels, restaurants, bakeries and cafes are filled with good things. The grocery stores and the monstrous grain elevators, where fortunes are made, and big buildings where provisions are stored, were noticed by her while wandering about, yet none of these offered any hope—there was FOOD

Betrayal

everywhere but not a crumb to save her from joining the countless number of the doomed.

Those only who have had the experience can realize the significance of finding oneself in a large city bereft of money and friends—it is simply maddening.

Night has overtaken her.

She is frightened, she is desperate; men ogle as they pass her.

She reached a street where all is commotion.

From all the houses, beautifully lighted, flow music and laughter.

She halts in front of one of these houses; she is dazed, she hasn't the courage to go further, she shudders and half turns away.

Men pass in groups and talk among themselves and fling jeering remarks at each other which were meant for her ears, and this frightens her all the more, and she wonders in which direction is the river. Rumbling of thunder is heard in the distance.

Just then a girl in a decollete dress and a rustling train, dragging a white scarf that she had grabbed in her haste, dashed out of

The Underworld Sewer

the basement door and as she reached the pavement, right in front of the shivering girl, she slipped on some orange peel and they both fell in a heap.

The crowd passing that way "roasted" them for being drunk, and the girl with the bare arms "fired" back an answer.

When the girls had scrambled upon their feet they apologized to each other.

The girl with the bare arms asked the stranger where she lived, who replied, "Out here in the street."

"Was your intention to come into one of these houses?"

"I see no other way," the stranger replied.

"I know just how you feel," responded the other; "I have been there myself. Well, come with me; I am going over to the corner saloon to get a package of cigarettes; they will hand them to me at the side door. I have got to hurry or they will miss me; I did not make it known to any one that I was going to step out, and the house is full of company. Besides, we will be caught in the rain."

Betrayal

It had begun to sprinkle, one thunder-clap after another rolled overhead. Clasping hands the girls began to run, and returned just in time to escape a drenching.

But when the girl with the stranger tried to go back the same way, through the basement door, they found it locked. The girl had broken a rule, and did not relish going to the front door, but was compelled to do so. As soon as the door opened the housekeeper exclaimed: "Oh here you are! We have been looking the house over for you." The girl with the bare arms explained her absence, and how she had run across the "new girl" who had come to stay.

"I will loan her some of my clothes until she can get a supply of her own," she said, as she lit a cigarette and left the "new girl" with the housekeeper.

If there is a redeeming feature in the underworld it is the humane treatment which the girls bestow upon each other.

They will loan clothing and money to each other, will tenderly wait upon each other during illness, and contribute the amount

The Underworld Sewer

necessary to pay doctor bills, or send a girl to a hospital, to her home, or pay funeral expenses. It seems that all girls who meet in the underworld from far or near are of the same temperament with regard to charity; nothing is too difficult or too valuable to sacrifice to relieve distress.

The underworld is noted for its generosity; the call to contribute to almost every fund by the Christian world, is always met with response, but which also presents a ludicrous side to the underworld, because of its moral inconsistency.

I refer to this to show that selfishness is not the sin of the underworld.

In the underworld, girls betrayed by lovers come from all classes of society and stages in life.

The daughter from the home of the poorest paid day laborer, from the home of the rich man, from the farmer's home, from the home of mechanics, from the home of the merchant, the banker, the preacher, the lawyer.

The daughters in all classes of homes are

Betrayal

caught in the toil of love by a man who is sowing his wild oats.

Neither riches nor poverty nor station in life protects the daughter from the boys or men who have not been taught self discipline.

Every girl is endowed by nature to respect, trust, confide in, love, worship and obey the man she loves.

Sacrifices on her part are a pleasure so long as she believes he is true to her, and treats her with the tenderness and kindness that is due her.

The school girl is captured by the kindness and attention of her schoolmate, or her neighbor's boy. She trusts him and depends upon him for protection, but by reason of having been taught that he must sow his wild oats he misleads her, and at the same time his good opinion of her diminishes, but it does not reduce the estimation of himself, because he has not been taught that way.

Yet this affair may blot the girl's whole life, and be the cause of recklessness that generally brings her sooner or later to the underworld.

TRUE AND UNTRUE

He was a dog,
  But he stayed at home
  And guarded the family night and day.
He was a dog
  That didn't roam.
  He lay on the porch or chased the stray—
  The tramps, the burglar, the hen, away.
  For a dog's true heart for that household beat
  At morning and evening, in cold and heat.
He was a dog.

He was a man,
  And didn't stay
  To cherish his wife and his children fair.
He was a man,
  And every day
  His heart grew callous, its love beats rare.
  He thought of himself at the close of the day
  And, cigar in his fingers hurried away
  To the club, the lodge, the store, the show,
  But he had a right to go, you know—
He was a man.

CHAPTER X.

Abandoned Wife

A man expects his wife to be an angel under any and all circumstances. The man pledges his protection, care and love for life, and upon these terms the woman becomes his wife, in full confidence that this love is permanent and lasting; in sickness or health she has a right to expect him to be true to her.

The greater burden of married life comes to the wife, who has her household duties, and the children to care for, and a thousand and one things to perform which make up the daily routine.

When the husband comes home from his daily occupation, his wife has a right to expect his company during the evening; to her his presence is company, even though he chooses to bury himself in his newspapers.

But she does not receive this consideration. He is absent night after night and often

Abandoned Wife

until the break of day, or for several days. When he arrives he is nervous and grouchy, and throws things around. While he is changing his wearing apparel he loses the proverbial collar buttons, strewing them upon the floor, and cussing because they are not as large as sledge-hammers. A man in that condition isn't noted for his nimble fingers among other deficiencies. His wife comes to his rescue, fastens his collar, and observes that his breath hasn't the aroma of violets, nor his blood-shot eyes the expression of remorse; he does not make the effort to hold his temper that he did the collar-button. With a scowl he tells his wife that he has been at a banquet.

He remains at home for a night or two to rest up. Then he goes to another banquet, or club, or he is called away from town on a matter of business, or important transactions kept him at the office, or he met some friends at the hotel who detained him; he volunteers this information without any interrogations from his wife, who trembles with fear that something is wrong. When men go out in bunches, they sometimes frankly admit to

The Underworld Sewer

their wives that they have been out with the boys seeing the sights, but THEY DON'T TELL WHAT THEY SAW; will occasionally TELL WHAT THE OTHER FELLOW DID, which has the tendency of making his wife suspicious of her own husband. But the man who is bent on going the pace, neglects his wife, which becomes more and more apparent; he grumbles and finds fault, he is selfish and unkind and abusive. Yet under all these conditions he demands that his wife shall continue to be an angel, while he lives a Dr. Jekyll and Mr. Hyde life, and regarding home as only a place to go when all other places are closed.

When she becomes a nervous wreck from failing health he is then ready to abandon her. This man has driven his wife to distraction.

Not even this angel could bear the burden his tyranny heaped upon her.

He is aware of what society, the law, justice and decency require of him.

But he is lost to all that. Nothing but sexual cravings and impulses fill his mind.

He takes his money to the public woman

Abandoned Wife

(the fairy) instead of taking it to his angel wife and the children.

The home is destroyed, the wife and family are abandoned, the husband goes his way in search of an "affinity," leaving his wife to support herself and the children the best way she can.

This is not imagination but true to life.

I have a particular instance in mind, which is one of many that came under my observation. A beautiful woman of only twenty-six years who was truly an angel wife as nearly as a woman could be, with five children to support, was deserted by her husband. Such cases are numbered by the thousands. But as to this particular case, after a long struggle with poverty the deserted wife and mother was driven to the underworld. It was the only means left for the support of her children.

She found a home for her brood, three in a family and two in a convent.

And then THIS ANGEL MOTHER WENDS HER WAY TO THE LAND THAT ATTRACTS MEN, to the land that men reserve for themselves, TO THE

The Underworld Sewer

LAND WHERE BEER, WINE AND TEARS FLOW LIKE WATER, and where MEN LAVISHLY SPEND THEIR MONEY in exchange for excitement. To the land where the many roads terminate, the gateway is always open, and all who enter are welcome.

Ah! It is said that "Greater love hath no man than this, that a man lay down his life for his friends." But it is not the hardest act to DIE for those we love, BUT TO LIVE IN DISGRACE, SELL BODY AND SOUL, and to devote a life to a condition where men expect us to take a part in all kinds of degradation for their entertainment, IN ORDER TO SUPPORT OUR CHILDREN, is a far GREATER SACRIFICE THAN DEATH.

Such a woman is always an angel ALTHOUGH she is in the midst of vice. Such a woman watches every ray of hope that may be the making of a home for herself and loved ones away from a life of sin.

Is it possible for you to comprehend that before such a woman can enter upon this life, the great mother love crowds out of mind

Abandoned Wife

for the time being all moral questions, honor, and reputation, considering only one object, the saving of her little ones. WHAT OTHER MOTHER HAS SACRIFICED SO MUCH? Under the present conditions SHE MUST FOREVER BE SEPARATED FROM ALL THAT IS GOOD, AND BE CROWDED DOWN FURTHER AND FURTHER DOWN. Is it any wonder that we are compelled to believe hard things of THOSE WHO PERMIT A CONDITION WHICH CONSIGNS A MOTHER TO SUCH A FATE?

There must be a system established under which a woman will not be driven to make this awful sacrifice. The present economic regulations, training and education must be eradicated, otherwise women's sacrifice will continue to be purchased in the market, cheaply, by men, RESULTING IN SORROW AND POVERTY FOR THEIR OWN WIVES AND CHILDREN, AND MOST DREADFUL DISEASE FOR THEMSELVES AND THEIR POSTERITY.

CHAPTER XI.

The Vampire

When a girl first arrives in the underworld she is termed a tenderfoot, a titbit, a chippy, and a new girl. Everybody is strange to her, and she is strange to everybody; and the opportunity to help initiate the strange one into the mysteries of the underworld is seldom overlooked by anybody.

Her past experience was only the beginning of her grief in comparison to the character which now awaits her. By the taunts, reproaches and ridicule, FOR THE BREACH OF UNDERWORLD ETIQUETTE, she is made most miserable. And when the P. I.* comes to force his attention upon her, she is almost sure to fall into the trap.

It depends to some extent upon what de-

---

* P. I. is an abbreviation for pimp; is used in the underworld as a milder term.

The Vampire

partment of the underworld happens to be her destiny; the lover may be found in all parts, but the MOST PERSISTENT AND BRUTAL are those in the lower crust.

The girl will not heed the advice to avoid the lover, preferring experience of her own.

And will grope along and try to study out the situation for herself.

If she happens to be wise, all the palaver of this human animal, the vampire, will fall upon the "desert air."

But more than half of the girls are entrapped by the professional P. I. If she can be convinced of his undying love, she becomes a willing victim. To her it means a companion with whom to converse in her awful loneliness.

Like her first betrayer, this man also holds out wonderful inducements, and through this ray of hope she imagines THERE MAY BE A CHANCE FOR REDEMPTION.

To love and be loved is a woman's leading characteristic. Whatever may be her lot, how much or how hard has been her experience

The Underworld Sewer

with men, she still lives in hopes that THIS ONE will be the exception.

At first this human vulture begins by borrowing her money; he never returns it as she believes he will do. She eventually begins to realize that she is supporting him. But by that time she is deeply in love with him.

When she has become "used to" supplying him with money, his demand for it is constant, and to urge its importance upon her, he emphasizes it with a beating. She will work hard then for some time. Money getting in the underworld is always termed WORK. Nothing can be more pathetic than this miserable slavery which must solve the bread and butter problem for her day by day.

To remind her of the depth of his love, and that he will "stand for no trifling," he punches her in the eye ever so often, breaks her nose, or a couple of ribs, or a limb, kicks her, stamps upon her, in fact wipes up the floor with her.

The Vampire

She seldom turns him over to the police, knowing that his punishment will be merely a fine, which is usually drawn from her own purse.

Some of these girls have not enough clothing to cover their bodies, because the vampire takes it as fast as she earns it; and she will also accept as a punishment the worst of beatings for not producing the money fast enough.

With all my observation this feature has been the most difficult to understand and explain.

The fact that a woman will select one man as her ideal, can be easier comprehended, as this is following out to some extent the bent of human nature.

Nature has made no provision for loving all men the same; this demonstrates that the LIFE OF THE WOMEN IN THE UNDERWORLD SEWER IS MOST UNNATURAL AND HORRIBLE.

But why is she willing to undergo the most

The Underworld Sewer

brutal punishment and abuse from the man she loves? Her condition as a rule does not appeal to sympathy; it is thought that one who would stand for such treatment does not deserve it. This is wrong, because she has no power over her action. The life she is leading has deprived her of the will power to escape, or even to desire to do so. Energy has become diseased or paralyzed, and she is in a pitiful state which is only possible to surmount by medical and moral applications.

This explanation comes as near to a reasonable solution as I can furnish, after a long and close observation.

The men who live upon women's earnings do not come from any special class.

They are those who are idle, and lazy, and dishonest, and ignorant. From this condition the professional P. I. emerges. Sometimes he has the appearance of a gentleman of fashion, with nothing to do but dress, and nothing to think of but to "while away the time" and to avoid the police. He wears the

The Vampire

best of attire and the most expensive jewels.

As you descend the scale of the underworld, you note that these vampires are provided with means according to the success they have in making their girls "dig up."

It must not be supposed, however, that all men who obtain money from the women are from the scum. The greatest number of lovers by far are NICE YOUNG MEN FROM MOST RESPECTABLE HOMES, who receive money regularly from these girls.

It is not the purpose of this book to deal with individuals, it would be a cowardly breach of confidence, otherwise we could unfold some marvelous truths.

It is not generally known that the MOST NUMEROUS LOVER in the underworld IS A RESPECTABLE MAN, in a respectable business.

If these men, who are of different ages and occupations, are KNOWN TO THE POLICE, they are NOT RECOGNIZED

The Underworld Sewer

AS LOVERS, because they are in legitimate business. But it is through money received from the women that makes it possible for them to be engaged in a legitimate business.

And occasionally a man KNOWS WHERE HE CAN OBTAIN A FINANCIAL LIFT IN A PINCH; this has been the making of many a rich man. MANY GREAT BUILDINGS HAVE BEEN ERECTED FROM MONEY THUS OBTAINED.

To be sure, these men do not beat their women, but they receive financial aid from them with regularity, and also get what is coming to them sooner or later.

If the RESPECTABLE UNDER-WORLD LOVER is receiving money in exchange for love, HE DOES NOT DIFFER MATERIALLY FROM THE LOWEST VAMPIRE, and is a lover as much as those who beat their women.

Not much principle could be expected to

The Vampire

have been developed in the man who has been raised in the slums.

But what shall we think of a MAN WHO IS EDUCATED and in good society AND OF SOUND MIND, who WILL TOUCH THIS POLLUTED MONEY? He is a culprit of modern production, WHICH SHOWS THE ABSENCE OF MORAL TRAINING, IN THE MIDST OF CULTURE.

After the man becomes diseased, and apparently cured, he then marries some respectable girl.

The idle vampire often does the same.

If a girl lives without any visible means of support in a respectable neighborhood the source of her living is soon questioned.

Not so with a man, who may live upon the earnings of these girls for years, and then, WITH ALL THAT DISEASE IN HIS BLOOD, marry an INNOCENT GIRL.

While the woman who has denied her-

The Underworld Sewer

self the necessities of life, and lived in the lowest depravity, that she might have money for this monster in human form—

THIS UNHAPPY GIRL ENDS ALL HER EARTHLY GRIEFS BY COMMITTING SUICIDE.

Suicide in the underworld is of such frequent occurrence that it does not attract the attention of the public unless there is something sensational about it.

CHAPTER XII.

The Assignation House

In department stores, and other establishments where girls are employed, they are surrounded by all kinds of temptations from their men customers, and often from the bosses and men employed in the establishment, who are also anything but real angels.

The girls dare not make it known, or ask for protection; to do so would be to lose their job.

Often they are accosted on the street and have requested a policeman for protection on these occasions, but have only received in return insinuation glances and interrogations. They can no longer regard the officer as a protector.

The girl to preserve her reputation must have a resolution of iron, and be ever on the alert for the decoy which may come garbed in so many different forms.

The Underworld Sewer

"Gentlemen that we meet in a business way," said a wage earner, "treat us so lovely and considerate as to inspire the greatest confidence and highest regard for them.

"It would be impossible for any of us to believe that a girl would be imperiled in the company of men with such refinement and generosity.

"But if a girl accepts an invitation to a show, to a supper or for an automobile ride, she will learn to her surprise the real meaning of his attentions. And they have such a gentlemanly way of telling us things," she said; "in fact, they will insult us in such a courteous way that a girl will at first refuse to believe her ears."

Such are the conditions which surround the wage earner.

Few girls have had the instruction that tends to prepare them to guard against the temptation when presented to them.

And when men pay them attention and flatter them they enter into a romantic flirtation which is meant to be harmless, but almost before they are aware of it THEY ARE IN THE DISTRICT.

The Assignation House

The other reason is the starvation wages on which they must exist, and is mainly responsible for the downfall of many of these girls, as it is often to add to their meager income which prompts this step. When the week's expenses are paid out of their income there is nothing left for clothing. All young girls long to be arrayed in the beautiful garments they see in the store and worn by customers. Who can blame a young girl for having these thoughts, especially when she observes the advantages which the girls with rich clothing seem to have, and she is told time after time by men who visit her counter that it is only a question of catching a man with money and every want will be supplied.

A man calls frequently at her counter to tell her this, and to purchase articles for which he has no use. But the object is accomplished; he escorts the girl to entertainments and then come the suppers, the first drink, and the downward road which leads to the assignation house.

It must be remembered that the assignation house is a source of supply and a branch of the underworld.

The Underworld Sewer

It is the channel through which the greater number of women come to the public house.

Innocent girls are constantly being deceived by all kinds of tricks to enter these houses, and in large cities they are even kidnaped by brutal men and brought to these houses, and sometimes compelled to earn money for them.

Here you will also find the adventuress and her lover and their blackmailing schemes.

But there are different varieties of assignation houses, some which the keepers do not designate by this name, but call it "renting rooms to couples," which they are particular about, and in some cases require these couples to furnish references, or be recommended by some one known to them.

The assignation house for the wealthy classes in the large cities is exceedingly profitable for the keeper.

It is very quiet, profoundly secluded and private.

It is where the husband of one woman meets the wife of his best friend, or the trusted bosom friend of his wife.

The Assignation House

It is where the bachelors in society meet the wives of men who are too busy making money to entertain their own wives.

The busy man comes to the underworld to be entertained when he has time, and also makes a business transaction of this, and does not linger by the wayside.

The keepers of these fashionable assignation houses never resort to blackmail, although they could divulge some terrible secrets by which thousands could be raked in as hush money.

The reason this is rarely ever done is because these keepers have a reputation of their own at stake. These places are for the rich to meet their affinities, and not for women who earn their living that way.

The class of assignation houses which is frequented by the clandestine women is found in abundance in large cities, and more or less in smaller ones.

There is always a strife between the clandestine woman who patronizes the assignation house and the public woman.

Each claiming that the other is leading the lower life of the two.

The Underworld Sewer

The private woman accuses the public woman of defying all decency, by her bold exhibitions, and that she is known accordingly, and must also receive the abuse of all kinds of men, "while we select our company and can go anywhere without attracting attention; we would not be one of you, NOT US." The professional woman has a thorough contempt for the "snap," whom she calls sly and dishonest and imposes upon respectability. The public woman claims she has not this sin to answer for in connection with many others; that she is in the business because she must earn her living that way, and when she quits the business, she QUITS, and "there is no two ways about it."

While these classes of women, who earn their living the same way, are distinctly different, the men who patronize them are no less so. Their occupation in the Christian world has nothing to do with it. They have their distinct and separate notions regarding their choice of these women. The man who supports the public women does not cultivate the acquaintance of the clandestine woman, and vice versa.

The Assignation House

All men have their reasons for their preference, and whether it be to have more safety as to their person and reputation, or more seclusion, their chances are the same.

THE CUSTOMER IS VERY UNINTERESTING TO EITHER CLASS of women unless they have the "wherewiths," if they but knew it.

CHAPTER XIII.

The Depth

At the bottom of the underworld can be found the lowest type of poverty stricken humanity; it is composed of all shades, grades and colors huddled together.

These places of existence are called cribs, dives, dens, holes, and nests, although they sometimes live in very pretentious looking houses. Here the thieves and murderers hang out. This property occupied by them may be owned by corporations, private companies or individuals; in either case they are civilized.

These hell-holes catch all kinds of girls on the drift, who do not realize their fate, or that they are with the scum of the earth, until too late. It would not be possible to escape even had they a desire to do so, nor does it take long to crowd out of existence, by such surroundings, any glimpse they have had of a better way of living.

The Depth

It is where male and female lie around everywhere stupefied with dope and liquor; the house is blue with smoke and profanity, and reeking in filth, disease and degradation.

In these dens in larger cities, where money is scarce and customers few, robbery and murders are most frequent. If a stranger happens to drop in among them he is quickly fleeced of his money and often the clothing he wears; if he escapes with his life he is fortunate.

Much of the influx to this living death we must admit is from drunken parents in large cities, who compel their children to furnish money by begging and stealing, and by debauchery of their daughters of tender age, whose parents and ancestors have lived in poverty and filth for centuries without education, training or nourishing food; dwarfed in body and mind, they are disqualified to earn a living except by vice.

The depravity in their nature is the result of a condition for which they are not responsible, but it is a breeding place for much of the worst of crime.

159

The Underworld Sewer

How can a tribe of intelligent beings blame them? The whole human family would be in the same predicament under similar conditions.

From these homes in the slums the girls are driven into the streets, and to these dives, where they are often picked up by men to be used as performers for their filthy, obscene shows, where humanity is exhibited in all its hideousness for money.

Men are always proprietors of these "SIGHTS," AND THE MORE VILE-LY AND INHUMANLY THEY ARE CONDUCTED, THE MORE PROFITABLE IS THE SHOW.

The proprietors usually become rich from them, while the degraded women performers are merely earning existence.

These establishments are maintained by patronage from the Christian world who pay a big admission fee to see these sights. SIGHTS too awful to be mentioned.

Men of means go there, men from all parts of the world go there; the greater part of men with these inclinations would not miss

The Depth

the opportunities of seeing the sights of a large city.

Among these men are our best citizens, who give as their reason for desiring to see them that they were "curious to know how low a woman could become."

They emerge from these places with distracted expressions and ejaculations of dismay! But the man (although he may not be one who mingles with the underworld) could no more resist seeing these SIGHTS than he could resist seeing a ball game or a horse race.

The average man reasons that all sights add to his knowledge; it does not occur to him that it fills his mind with loathsome thoughts which he will never wholly blot out, not to mention the loss of confidence in the human race, which no man of intelligence can escape.

Men seldom report the details of the horrors they see in these places. If complaint has ever been entered against the proprietors, it has fallen on barren soil, as no one has ever heard of it. As a rule the authorities know

The Underworld Sewer

about these sights and how they are conducted; and, you may be sure, profit by them.

In fact in some cities you can get a guide at police headquarters to show you the sights, and if you are a good fellow, and slip him a "V" or "X," he will take pains to escort you to the right places, for which you will congratulate yourself for having got your money's worth. All of these establishments are run by MEN for money and patronized by MEN for curiosity.

Through the greed and avarice of men, who saw in the depraved condition of these unfortunate girls a chance to put them on exhibition for profit and literally sell this depravity to men who crave such amusement, these performers who are required to furnish the entertainment are not to blame, as they know nothing about morals.

The men who have come to see these girls perform in these obscene shows would not give them a crust of bread, a pleasant smile, or a thought of pity.

These girls do not feel any timidity; they have never had any. They have only an in-

The Depth

stinct for self-preservation, and regard the visitors merely as a herd of cattle, which is wrong of course, as the comparison is a slander on the animals.

Vice is a valuable commodity to some men and they will pay extravagant prices for it, and the women must exhibit and sell the condition which has the value in exchange for a living.

Of what use is education and the higher attainments if it only inspires a desire to gloat over depraved humanity? The sight-seer is morally on a lower scale than the unfortunate women. Are men burdened with too much education, too little, or not the right kind?

These perverted men who are so eager to see depraved objects, are just as much in need of reform as the girls they hire in different ways.

What does the sightseer say about the show and performers?

"Oh! what low creatures!"

What do they say about the proprietor?

There is no answer; he has not been considered.

The Underworld Sewer

WHAT DO THEY SAY ABOUT EACH OTHER for paying big money to see "the children of the trough" of civilization EXHIBIT THEMSELVES IN THE LOWEST FORM OF DEGRADATION FOR THEIR ENTERTAINMENT, WHERE THE WICKEDEST AND MOST DEGENERATE OF HUMAN THOUGHTS ARE EXPRESSED IN PERSONATIONS? All is silence.

This DEGRADATION CAN NOT BE DESCRIBED IN WORDS, and should not be if it were possible.

IT IS ALLOWED BY THE MEN of this proud nation TO EXIST, to satisfy the lowest, meanest propensities of mankind.

CHAPTER XIV.

The First Drink and the Saloon

This first drink is never obtained in saloons but supplied in homes, private dining halls, hotels, restaurants and cafes.

The first drink can also be traced to the soda fountain in drug stores, where it may be obtained without attracting any attention. It would never occur to a girl to take a drink of liquor, unless in company with a man WHO URGES HER, and DARES HER TO DO SO, which she will do, especially if she is interested in the man.

The liquor habit is so interwoven with the underworld that it is impossible to explain our condition without bringing into notice one of the chief causes which applies directly to the social evil.

The public dance hall is one of the starting points, and the broad road that leads to

The Underworld Sewer

the assignation house. At these halls there are no restrictions upon a man; he may imbibe as much as he pleases between dances and there is no one to restrain him from urging his partner to drink from a bottle which he often carries in his pocket.

The girls who attend these dances are those who are employed somewhere; they go there for recreation; sometimes they have no escorts, depending upon their chance acquaintance for their entertainment. These girls are not bad, just "green," unsophisticated; they do not realize any danger.

The clandestine woman will attend these BALLS TO BECOME ACQUAINTED FOR FINANCIAL PURPOSES. The underworld woman will go if she can conceal her identity; she goes for recreation, too, but it usually terminates in her expulsion, by reason of becoming "tanked up" on the contents of somebody's bottle.

The men who come to these dances may be from any branch of society, from the highest to the lowest; they don't all go to pick up a girl, but SUCH IS THE SURROUND-

The First Drink

INGS OF THE GOOD GIRL WHO IS EMPLOYED and must depend upon something of this nature for her relaxation from toil.

Many of our girls can trace the cause of the first step downward to the first drink urged upon her at one of these public dances, by some young man who may be from the upper or lower crust of society. Liquor makes cowards of brave men, and brave men of cowards, so brave and reckless as to attack the innocent girl with greater success.

These two awful evils, the bad man and the bad drink, each of which muddles the mind and is the first danger signal which the girl on the road should heed.

Although the saloon is mostly the gateway through which men visit the underworld, it is not directly responsible for the woman's FIRST DRINK.

Most girls who arrive in the underworld have not yet become habitual users of liquor of any kind. But most of them will acquire the habit quickly.

There are all kinds of inducements for

The Underworld Sewer

girls to become drunkards, as it is sold in all houses and in all departments of the underworld, and the girls are required to drink, or "ditch it," in order to keep up the expenses of the "house."

In fact the greatest profit is made on the beer and wine sold, and if the landlady becomes wealthy, it is mostly through this channel it is accomplished.

There is also an OUTSIDE influence that aids in making drunkards of our girls.

It is drink, drink, DRINK for the girls in the sewer from night till morning, and from morning till night.

There are a few who try to save themselves by drinking only when they are compelled to do so to obtain the money "in sight."

But most of our girls become drunkards. If they are not drinking with customers, they are out buying drinks, which is not obtainable in saloons, but there are many places reserved for our girls.

Our temperance lecturers claim that the taste for liquor in all cases is an acquired habit. This is nowhere more thoroughly verified than in the underworld.

The First Drink

I have watched both men and women force the stuff down their throats and shudder; I have observed the same persons later smack their lips with relish; I HAVE SEEN THEM BECOME BLOATED, BLEAR-EYED AND UNSIGHTLY CREATURES.

The saloon is a preparatory department in the school of social evil; all cities that issue license are accomplices, as it gives power to stunt, dwarf and corrupt the minds and bodies of their citizens, that the money may go through this channel to the school funds and to build up your cities. It is a wonderful system which is able to make the SAME MONEY SERVE TWO PURPOSES, THAT OF DEGRADING AND EDUCATING.

The license-voters are not always those who patronize the saloon, but they are always those who are benefited by the same, or else why do they vote that way? MEN, GOOD MEN, who come to our houses, MUST FIRST TAKE A DRINK in the saloon in order to have THE NERVE TO

169

The Underworld Sewer

COME; MANY WOULD OTHER-
WISE NOT COME.

Very few men come to the underworld
unless under the influence of liquor more or
less.

All men who buy liquor, poor or rich, sup-
port the saloon, BUT THE POOR MEN
WHO PATRONIZE THE SALOON
ARE NOT THE MEN WHO MAKE
THE WHEELS GO AROUND IN
THE UNDERWORLD.

Regular patrons of the saloon and
SEWER always take their "personal liberty" BRACER BEFORE COMING;
they have voted to keep things moving on
account of business and other interests.

It is customary to attack the saloon proprietor with all kinds of rancor, even though
he is in a legal business made so by the law.

Instead of the abuse and browbeating en-
mity of the man, THERE IS THE
CAUSE of the traffic, which awaits all this
activity.

The saloon keeper's job is not an enviable
one; he is a target for every shark who represents the law.

The First Drink

Drains upon his generosity are of daily occurrence; politicians and police, who pretend to be friends, by extending favors, or pretending to do so, expect and are supplied with free cigars and drinks regularly, and money which is most often never returned.

He is imposed upon in various ways which he can not expose. When he is on duty he is merely an automatic machine, and can not stop to consider insults.

He does not enjoy the position of being AMONG A LOT OF DRIVELING IDIOTS, as most men are when under the influence of drink, and could not stand the strain except for the fact that he is earning a living for himself and family.

The saloon keeper is a most generous fellow; those who come to him for the church donation, or the hobo hand-out, are never turned away empty-handed. Under that rough exterior beats a warm heart, is generally admitted.

When a realization occurs that liquor is not needed for any purpose whatever, it will be revealed how it may be abolished without

The Underworld Sewer

abusing the people engaged in carrying on the evil which you have voted for.

The DISGRACE OF THE LIQUOR EVIL SHOULD FALL UPON MEN, WHO BY THEIR VOTES MAKE IT POSSIBLE AND ALSO NECESSARY for an individual to follow such an occupation.

I stand for the universal prohibition of the liquor traffic, and from my point of view, from the underworld, I can substantiate every argument produced by the temperance workers. Liquor is for no other purpose than to make beasts of men and women, and to keep money in circulation. I believe that every effort should be made, by voters and non-voters, to prevail upon Uncle Sam, the MOST POWERFUL SUPPORTER OF THE SALOON, to help deliver the slaves of liquor from their bondage. MEN OR WOMEN IN ANY PART OF THE COUNTRY ARE PRIVILEGED TO SECURE A GOVERNMENT LICENSE TO DISPENSE LIQUOR, ALL THAT IS NEEDED IS THE

172

The First Drink

PRICE TO PAY FOR THE REVENUE. THE GOVERNMENT DOES NOT CONCERN ITSELF IN THE DESTRUCTION IT CAUSES. But if an individual has not PAID FOR THE PRIVILEGE, WOE BE TO HIM OR HER. *Women's suffrage would make the right change.* I have never taken up this question, but all my life I have wondered at the monumental gall of men for not permitting this bill to pass; they no doubt KNOW that there would be SOMETHING DOING THAT THEY DON'T WANT DONE. NO RIGHTS SHOULD BE DENIED THE MOTHERS OF OUR NATION.

A most encouraging sign of the times is the fact that the injury produced upon the human body by the use of intoxicating drinks is being taught in a mild way in some of our public schools.

So far the teaching is handled with gloves, but the principle involved is that which leads to prohibition.

The Underworld Sewer

If this could be boldly taught in all schools and intelligently drilled into the children in the homes, the next generation would not tolerate the liquor traffic. This, united with other remedies which may be applied now, will effectually squelch it.

"Refuse to take the first drink," is the advice of the prohibitionists; I echo the same advice. The dance hall or Sunday dance, where the promiscuous collection of people meet, are harmful in all ways. Places of amusement should be provided which will furnish protection for the girls who are employed.

Refuse to take the first drink, is used in the arguments to avoid a drunkard's grave; but I have never heard of the argument being made to girls and women as a safety against landing in the underworld.

The young people do not take a serious view of drinking, regarding it only as being sporty; and this is a term which carries with it considerable inflation, with the very young man; he enjoys having this said of him.

Protect those who can not protect them-

The First Drink

selves, says the prohibitionist, and from my corner I say, AMEN.

The only mistake that prohibition makes is that it treats the liquor traffic as an evil within itself when in reality it is one of the features of an evil system, and to win a complete victory prohibition must direct all of its strength toward changing the system.

CHAPTER XV.

The Madam

The madam or the landlady of a public house occupies the station in the underworld corresponding to the owners or managers in the establishments of the business world.

The woman becomes a madam just as a man becomes a manager, boss, or an owner, by progression or chance.

To a great extent it depends upon her qualifications.

Her inclinations may be good, or they may be bad, according to her disposition and intelligence.

The successful boss is the one who commands obedience without unnecessary display of authority; one who can make things come her way without domineering.

She knows when to be indulgent, and when the firmness that amounts to harshness must be applied.

176

The Madam

The successful madam must not lose the confidence of those she is directing and managing; if so, she loses prestige, and loses control of her house.

In the underworld the landlady must not take her mind off her business for a minute.

She is responsible for everything, and is quick to detect any turmoil among customers and girls; and it depends upon her promptness in adjusting and subduing the disturbance, to prevent consequences.

The wise matron of the underworld is a woman of many resources and sound judgment, which is gained by experience so severe that you would not believe it possible for a human being to endure.

She is judge and jury and settles every dispute arising in her house.

It is care and anxiety, fear, sorrow and dread, continually from the first to the last chapter, with the matron who assumes the full charge of her house.

The large palaces keep a retinue of servants, who answer the "rings," escort each party to separate rooms, order the beer or

The Underworld Sewer

wine which is served upon a solid silver tray by one of the colored maids. There are two housekeepers, one for day and one for night. The landlady is never called upon except in extreme cases.

The day housekeeper pays the servants, keeps the books and settles with the girls and takes full charge.

In these houses you see the glaze of diamonds and jewels of the most costly kind upon customers and occupants.

These houses are furnished in grand magnificence, from the exquisite dining room to the remotest nook.

But life for the girls, surrounded by all this grandeur, is not an easy one; BENEATH IT ALL ARE UNTOLD SORROW AND MISERY.

Upon the first arrival of the girl, she imagines that all her troubles will be gone when she becomes acquainted with the rich man, but there is no class of men who are less generous than the rich man when he is sober, although he will spend thousands of dollars for self-indulgence, buying cham-

The Madam

pagne by the case. He will order all that
the bunch can drink, waste, lave and wallow
in.

The girls are required to take a part in
the lowest debauchery, for the amusement of
this man, for which they are liberally supplied with money, besides the madam's rake-
off isn't small; through all kinds of confu-
sion she never loses sight of the business part
of it.

After a girl has been through one of these
ORGIES with THE RICH MAN,
THERE IS NOTHING LEFT IN
THE LINE OF VICE THAT IS NOT
FAMILIAR TO HER.

A girl might be in some parts of the un-
derworld for years, and not have the knowl-
edge or experience IN VICE that THESE
GIRLS HAVE LEARNED UNDER
THE DIRECTION OF ONE RICH
MAN, IN A WEEK OR A MONTH'S
EXTREME REVELRY.

Hundreds of rich men are entertained in
this way daily in these houses.

The servants who are employed in these

179

The Underworld Sewer

magnificently furnished palaces are required
to attend strictly to their duties and be respectful to all, and close their eyes and
mouths to all sights and sounds.

In the smaller houses the landlady assumes control of her house with few servants.

The landlady of the underworld is usually
misrepresented.

She is accused of illtreating the girls in
various ways, by "locking them in" and
"overcharging," etc. You will find ignorant and abusive managers in all branches of
business, and it isn't to be supposed that the
underworld business is an exception.

As a rule the landlady is kind to the girls,
and if she has been obliged to "lock her in,"
it is usually to the advantage of the girl, who
has a vagabond designer waiting around the
corner for a piece of money, or to go away
with her on a drunken spree, which is sure
to land the girl in jail.

Professional writers will often attempt
to explain the inward workings of a public
house, but they make a dismal failure of it,
to say the least.

The Madam

If a girl has become involved in a frenzied affair over some good-for-nothing dope-fiend, who is obtaining all of her money, in such case the madam may try to detain her any old way, as the occasion warrants severe measures. It is regarded in the underworld as the proper thing to use these restrictions to break up the combination.

Besides, it is always a reflection upon the "reputation" of the landlady and her house for ITS MEMBERS TO BE ARREST-ED; THE DISGRACE AND HUMIL-IATION ARE NOT DIMINISHED BY THE FREQUENT REPETI-TION.

These underworld "crooks" who live upon the girls belong to the lowest grade of humanity, and it is the duty of the landlady to protect her girls from them as much as possible.

The landlady is the BEST FRIEND THE GIRL HAS, AND IT IS GEN-ERALLY SO ADMITTED by the girl who believes in being anywhere near decent; the girl depends upon the madam's

The Underworld Sewer

judgment and will come to her for advice in all her troubles; in fact, there is a GOOD WILL AND LOVE BETWEEN THEM THAT NOTHING CAN CHANGE.

During my many years as one of the girls, I was never restricted by locks by any madam, and I have lived in different houses from coast to coast.

And during the time I managed a public establishment I never made a prisoner of a girl; I never found it necessary; if I could not influence her by the different ways that are known to me, I preferred to let the girl have her experience, as sooner or later she is awakened to the man's motive. If he has not succeeded in making her as depraved as himself, she will eventually realize that the landlady was her best friend. The madam, who has had all of this experience, knows how to appreciate the girl's position.

It is generally supposed that when the girl gives up "the little independence that street life affords" and comes to the madam, that it is greatly to her disadvantage. While

The Madam

there is no such thing as independence in any branch of the underworld, least of all can it be applied to the women on the street. Under the care of the madam, she will at least be somewhat protected.

It must be remembered that the "madam," "landlady" or "house" will not be upheld by any court in restraining a girl from leaving the house whether she be in debt or not; nor to hold her clothes as security, unless the madam has a good stand-in with the politicians and police who are in power, the courts will not settle the trouble in the underworld —SO THE UNDERWORLD MUST HAVE AND ENFORCE SOME LAWS OF ITS OWN.

The madam is often accused of taking the greater share of the earnings of her boarders, WHICH IS NOT TRUE; the decent madam would not rob the girls of their small share, neither would the department stores take the earnings of their employes—BUT THE GREATER PROFIT IS ABSORBED BY THE HOUSE.

There is quite a similarity in that respect

The Underworld Sewer

in the method pursued in the business world and in the UNDERWORLD SEWER.

For instance, the department stores must realize off their girls, who transact the business of the house and earn the money which makes the profit. And no matter how unreasonable the customer may be, nor how much their patience and temper are taxed, they must appear outwardly serene and pleasant to their customers.

They must be neat, and they must work full time, be honest, and turn in all the money they shall collect.

The house keeps tab on their allowance for service until pay day, and if the girl is entitled to more than her regular contract, it is paid to her.

The contract is such as the HOUSE FIXES, AND THE GIRL MUST ACCEPT IT IF SHE WORKS.

There is no dishonesty about it, as the business world looks at it, because the house keeps its contract faithfully.

However, the HOUSE KNOWS HOW MUCH THE GIRL CAN SELL—

The Madam

ALSO KNOWS HOW LITTLE SHE CAN MANAGE TO EXIST UPON; also knows what the profit will be upon the goods she must sell to hold her job.

However, the contract is based upon the amount which (together with the assistance which she may be able to obtain from other sources) will permit her to exist.

The house will not for a moment consider the profit which comes in from her labor as a factor in fixing the amount of her salary.

The department store keeps the girl until she is compelled to sacrifice her honor in order to hold her job, or until she becomes disgraced, and when she loses her position, she comes to the madam, who arranges with her somewhat upon a similar basis, except that her ability to get assistance from any other source can not be considered, because there is no way for her to do so. But on the contrary, if anything in the way of assistance is given, she will have a lover for whom she is sacrificing her soul.

Neither the department store nor the madam cheats the girls, but in each case the

The Underworld Sewer

HOUSE GETS MOST OF THE PROFIT.

ONE IS JUST AS BAD AS THE OTHER, IF NOT A LITTLE WORSE. In fact, the department store drives the girl to the madam by paying her as little as possible, and the madam tries to keep the girl by the same means.

The financial difference of the two HOUSES is that THE MERCHANT BECOMES A MILLIONAIRE by the efforts of THE GIRLS EMPLOYED, while BUT FEW of the underworld establishments even become wealthy.

But all large undertakings in the business world where girls are employed rake off an enormous profit earned by their employes, without making a fair division.

The majority of madams do not stop to consider the immorality of their business. If she stops to think about it at all, she decides that the world would soon give her the "cold shoulder" if she did not have the money to pay her way.

To her it is merely a BUSINESS, a dis-

186

The Madam

agreeable, disreputable business, which she hates. Her PLANS are to RETIRE when SHE HAS MONEY ENOUGH TO LIVE UPON.

So the madam, the same as the girl, postpones the quitting time from year to year.

It is a difficult task for her to QUIT THE BUSINESS WHICH PAYS SO WELL.

Neither the madam nor the girls are responsible for the conditions they are in.

CHAPTER XVI.

One Night

It is the week of the state fair, or a big political doings, or a fraternity meeting, or a convention night; this is our harvest time.

Old and young, drunk and sober, are at the door awaiting admission.

There are whole jags, and half jags by the score.

Those who are boisterous, bold and daring, and the timid who wish to avoid being seen.

Crowd after crowd come to the different doors and yell for admission.

They are drunk, we fear them; WE NEVER GET OVER THIS FEAR, although we have seen the same performances daily year after year.

A drunken bunch have arrived, they are young and handsome fellows, they use vile language. We designate them as "Smart-Alecks," or "Arabs," because there is no

One Night

limit to their audacity. They are society dudes and imagine they are making a hit with our girls, by exhibiting their toughness, and failing to find an appreciative audience, they pinch and hurt the girls just to hear them scream, and curse and call them names, if they try to protect themselves; this produces a "red-headed" effect upon all of us, which means that the Arabs must "skidoo."

We have the reputation of leading young men into vice, but to hear the language used by these young Arabs would soon convince you that we could not teach them anything in this line.

The next visitors are hilarious in the extreme; they push, leer, crowd against each other in the hallway and march to the tune of a vile song; they demand beer, which we furnish; they sing more songs of smut, and order more beer at a dollar a bottle. The same quality may be purchased at the corner saloon for a quarter, but to a drunken man the expensive kind has the better flavor, and, then they have an audience consisting of pretty girls to hear them tell their stories and

189

The Underworld Sewer

to laugh at them. Soon these people drop out, and the house is refilled by different crowds. This time they are fine looking fellows with badges pinned on the lapel of their coats.

They treat us considerately and kindly; they are very anxious not to be seen by the other crowds in the various rooms, and the various crowds in the different rooms are very anxious not to be seen by them.

And so we oblige them, and protect them against their own friends.

They ask for beer in all parlors, and we serve it at once.

They are beginning to tell jokes everywhere. The jokes we have heard before, but we laugh; this is one of the parts we are required to learn to act when we first enter the underworld.

They drink more beer and tell more stories with whiskers upon them. They ask for a dancer; a girl is found who can supply their demand, and whether it be a jig or a rag, or a hoochee-koochee, it amuses them extremely, and whether the music is furnished

One Night

by a box, or a cracked piano, or a poll-parrot like phonograph, it is all the same, and is very inspiring and in harmony with the occasion.

And sometimes a dignified member of the badge crowd will join in the dance, and after they drink some more beer, THEY WILL ALL join in. And then there is a lot of laughter, and a lot more beer and stories with whiskers a mile long.

In their merrymaking they have forgotten about the other crowds in the house, until the door is pushed open and a familiar voice is heard to say, "I did not think you fellows frequented these places," and the reply is, "The same right back at you," and then they shake hands, and a lot more beer is ordered.

Then someone suggests that it is getting late, and they file out; just about this time the crowd in the next room take a notion to go and come rushing out in the hall only to meet the very friends they were trying to avoid.

Sometimes they fear each other's discretion, and other times they are political oppo-

The Underworld Sewer

nents and do not wish to meet each other under these circumstances, but the fear vanishes after the beer has been passed around liberally.

Well! such laughter! such yelling and exclamations! and then they all return in a bunch to one room, and have more beer and more dancing, in which nearly all join, and for a few minutes bedlam seems to have been let loose, in which we all join and laugh in REAL EARNEST.

If there is anything that is real amusing it is to see these stately, dignified gentlemen dance the "cake-walk."

And then they all grab their hats and disappear.

All this time there has been ringing, rapping, pounding from the outside for admission. Other branches of the badge crowd continue to come all the evening.

We again open the doors to as many as the house can hold and escort them to the different parlors.

Among them is a crowd of "good fellows" who yell for beer as soon as they reach the room; we supply them.

One Night

These fellows don't ask for dancers; they do their own dancing, in fancy quick-steps, which they do gracefully and well. All we have to do to get their money is to watch them, and applaud, which we never omit.

It does not occur to them that it is a part of our business to make it appear that we never saw such wonderful dancing.

The beer comes fast, and the dancing continues; the house is dense with smoke; more beer!

These GOOD FELLOWS do not cease dancing until they are exhausted, and then go.

As soon as there is a vacant parlor it is re-filled at once; there is calling for beer all over the house, and they are supplied as fast as possible.

Here come our Dutch friends, we are immediately handed a handful of silver dollars at the door, with the information, "wer sind sehr durstig." Their looks would not indicate it, however.

While we are spending the money they have given us, they sing all the songs they

The Underworld Sewer

know, in Dutch, and are amusing themselves trying to teach the girls to sing "Du wise nicht wie gut ich tehr ben, JA JA," etc. When a Dutchman is out drinking with friends he always uses his native language, although he speaks the English language with ease.

After drinking all the "peer" they can hold they take their departure, but always return to get that "schonen medchen" to dance for them just once more.

Among the parties that we unintentionally admit is a bunch of students, to whom we have talked with "tears in our eyes," urging them to stay away from such places.

But after having called at one or two of the saloons along the line, they come, and one of their maneuvers is to send some one to the door unknown to us, and the balance of the crowd line up against the wall or keep out of sight until the door is open, and then they all file in. After they are in, we let them remain long enough to talk a few minutes. They do not part their hair in the middle, or have a lock hanging down in their

194

One Night

eyes. They do not blackguard in our presence. They are wholesome, manly and courteous. There is no use in being anything but frank with them, as they have no money to spend. We sometimes take time to discuss political economy with them and find them liberal and broad in their ideas, and we look for much improvement when it shall fall upon them to take part as leaders.

The crowds are constantly coming and going, and all drink beer and tell smutty stories, dance occasionally a two step and waltz with the girls.

The saloons are now closed, and a proprietor with some of his club friends have arrived, and we make haste to reserve a parlor for them. The wise saloon keeper does not drink until after business hours; they are money spenders when they come down the line, which is not often, but they treat us with great consideration, and do not monopolize our time, but drink beer and tell stories and jokes among themselves, if occasion demands. Here is where the girls are supplied with gratuitous donations.

195

The Underworld Sewer

The house is now filling up with crowds who are very tired and awfully drunk. They all call for beer at the same time, which we serve as fast as possible; any lagging brings a volley of oaths. Their songs, their stories and their beer buying does not vary from the former callers, but these crowds are drunk, ugly, and abusive.

All of our judgment which we have stored up from years of experience is called into action to keep rows down, which means a strain upon our nerves and activity in the severest sense.

If a public house permits rows to occur a few times, we get the reputation of conducting a TOUGH PLACE; for this reason we do not allow one to happen, if it can be avoided.

At intervals during the night there are timid customers coming singly or in pairs—who buy what they want and go.

There is a steady coming and departing of these silent customers, who are of different ages.

It is now 4 o'clock a. m., and time to close. All the rooms upstairs have been rented.

One Night

But there is still violent ringing of the house bell. We explain that we have no room, we have closed for the night, etc.; they curse and hurl vile epithets at us, and continue to push the bell, so we turn the switch that cuts the ringing off.

There are still different parties in the house who have asked permission to remain until train time, and promise to make it profitable.

We are all so tired, but we submit. One of the crowds has some trained singers in their party, and the singing they produce is worthy of a better place. And as we listen to the singing, we are carried AWAY OFF somewhere—where the surroundings are clean—and we hope that we will never return. Oh, what longings for home and friends of long ago it brings to us, and we only wish it would last forever!

But we can not dream long at a time in the underworld; we are brought back to our senses and surroundings with a THUD by these beautiful songs, turning into this one, "How dry I am, how dry I am, and no one

The Underworld Sewer

seems to give," etc., and then we bring them something for their throats. The bunch in the next room have just started a burlesque on the professional singing they have overheard; this is so ridiculous and amusing that the singers send them some beer to keep them quiet.

Morning is dawning, and one of the guests announces that it is near train time, so the stories, jokes and beer must come fast. The girls come downstairs one by one for a few minutes to help herd the cattle.

Fast come the stories and jokes, and faster comes the beer midst dense cigar and cigarette smoke and loud laughter. And the next room crowd will not keep quiet; they are all singing a different tune at the same time, which begins to sound like cats of different varieties and every living thing in the barnyard had been let loose for a jubilee-meeting.

Finally one by one the herds go. And the noisiest ones are last, and when they reach the door and find it is daylight, it calls for another uproarious song, "We won't go home till morning."

One Night

As the madam is locking the doors a girl comes downstairs, she staggers as she walks, she wants a bottle of beer; upon refusal, she begs for "just this one," so it is given to her, and while making change for the bill the girl has brought to pay for the beer, the madam observes a lot of money in the cash drawer—how she hates it! She is conscious that it has been, and is, and will continue to be, the cause of all sin, and the curse of humanity. There is a big pile of it in the drawer. "Have we been paid for the work we have done tonight?" she asks herself. "Can money pay us for the work we do here? Can all the wealth in the world pay us for what we are doing? How would it be to throw it into the street? No! it buys our food. How would it be to commit suicide? No! for that would be murder. Then, my God, what shall I do? Show me a way," she prays, "to leave it all behind."

In answer to a ring at the back door, she goes and admits the servants, and as she steps past them into the cool, fresh air of the dawn of a new day, she wonders how long

The Underworld Sewer

it will take the OTHER DAWN to reach the underworld. In her musings she asks, "Why are we here? What are we here for? For the privilege of existing?" "Surely this can not be the mission of any human being!" "Yet I have been told several times during the past night that such houses MUST exist, for the protection of society." "Who!" "Or WHAT IS this society, that demands human souls and bodies for stepping-stones?"

"These men from the Christian world come to be entertained, they come to enjoy themselves, they come to make us their slaves, they come to tell filthy stories and sing songs of the same nature. And to require the daughters and sisters of other men to join them in the chorus; they come to empty their filth that is in their minds into the souls of the daughters and sisters of other men."

"They come to demand of the daughters and sisters of other men to appear before them in the richest gowns, or in the nude, as their particular taste may suggest, and to dance and jest for their entertainment."

One Night

"The best of men, AS THE WORLD SEES THEM, come to our houses for the single purpose of satisfying the lust of their bodies; the worst of men come for the same reason."

"If we don't like either of the propositions, to accept the money or starve, we still have one more chance of relief, which is suicide. Such is the condition that society INDORSES AS A NECESSITY, but it is too IMMACULATE TO HEAR ABOUT."

And thus she stands and soliloquizes until ready to fall from want of sleep, before she seeks repose.

This is a tempered description of one night, which is, with some variations, the description of every night in every town or city when there is a crowd in town, and at all other times there is a steady traffic.

A woman of our kind is not always the hardened creature she is represented to be. They say about her that she is a drunken, foul-mouthed, debased creature, whose face is so thick with paint that it would be im-

The Underworld Sewer

possible to see her blush if she ever had such an inclination.

When a woman is debased, hardened and low, SHE IS WHAT MEN AND CONDITIONS HAVE MADE HER.

The language we hear from men is revolting and degrading beyond description. There is no language too rotten, too foul, for men to use in our presence.

We use PAINT for two reasons; first, because MEN ADMIRE IT, or they would not come within reach of us, and then it ANSWERS AS A MASK TO HIDE BEHIND, to shield our tortured feelings from the savages who defile the air with their hideous language.

It would be more of a gratification to these brutes if they could but see the trembling and shuddering and blushing behind the mask.

The foul language they use is meant to HURT US, to WOUND US with the VENOM of REPTILES.

It is not surprising that some girls become foul-mouthed and use the lessons they have

One Night

been taught to whip and lash their torment-ors.

A more surprising feature is that any of them can hold themselves above it, for the underworld women all come under the same training.

In all parts of the underworld, this revolt-ing language is used by the drunken men from the Christian world.

The average underworld woman is a **MOST TIMID CREATURE**, made so by ill-treatment.

CHAPTER XVII.

Fairy and Victim

Men often call us their fairies.

They never seem to discover their mistake until they exhaust their money.

The successful woman in money earning must at all times and under all circumstances appear to be a fairy, and sometimes assume queenly airs to suit the occasion.

In fact, the underworld woman must be an actress, and those who act their part well are the most successful financially.

Man has by deception robbed us of our reputation; we have by deception learned how to obtain his money without robbing him.

As soon as we LEARN OUR DE-PLORABLE CONDITION, we have learned the lesson of PRETENDED PROTECTION and the LESSON OF PRETENDED LOVE.

204

Fairy and Victim

As soon as we REALIZE our condition, our confidence in men has fled.

We are awakened to the fact that WE CAN MANAGE THE MEN in the same way THEY MANAGED US.

With bitter resentment a girl will retaliate on men.

The treacherous treatment she has received from him incites in her a feeling of revenge. She pays him back in his own coin.

In other words, he gets it "back in the neck, and then some."

The weapons which men use to bring women to the underworld are in turn used by her to maintain her mortal existence.

HER SUCCESS depends upon her capacity to USE SIMILAR TACTICS to those which the men used to accomplish her ruin.

Men are easy subjects to the women who understand the ways of the underworld, and FALL INTO THEIR OWN TRAP QUITE READILY.

When a woman has been in the business a while she learns to give the customer

The Underworld Sewer

WHAT HE WANTS, but which he is never looking for, namely, "PLENTY OF TAFFY," she does not spare him.

The woman who has become a public fairy makes believe she loves her customer, and, singular as it may seem, THE MORE IN-SINCERELY SHE DEALS WITH HIM, the better hit she produces.

When he takes his departure he is in bliss-ful ignorance that HE IS RIDICULED AS SOON AS THE DOOR IS CLOSED. And yet he may be a regular customer for years.

The only thing that a man has of any value to a BUSINESS WOMAN in the underworld is HIS MONEY.

We haven't any REGARD FOR HIM IN OUR HEARTS, knowing that he has left a loving and trustful wife at home, WHO IS COUNTING THE MIN-UTES OF HIS ABSENCE.

We know of what we are speaking, HAV-ING BEEN ON BOTH SIDES OF THE CURTAIN.

Is it not strange that a man (with a loving

Fairy and Victim

wife at home) can feel proud of himself when we MAKE HIM BELIEVE THAT HE IS THE EXCEPTION, and the favorite one among all men; and THAT WITH ALL OUR WIDE OPPORTU-NITIES, we love him most.

He comes to us and we PILE UP OUR DECEPTION about as HIGH as he can STACK UP HIS MONEY. A vain man is easily managed. But even the most cul-tured and sedate man is susceptible to flat-tery when it appeals to a particular achieve-ment or trait from which he draws his pride. A woman will quickly discover his weak points, and that he is not adverse to listening to all her arts and blandishments, which she proceeds to spread out to his heart's content. It is astonishing how much gush a man can stand, no matter how raw it is applied; he believes he is entitled to it all. There is a commodity on which Wall Street sometimes gambles, as well as uses to express extreme cajolery. I refrain from using it out loud, but it would express the deal men get in the underworld. Does he get "Miked"? I guess,

The Underworld Sewer

yes, and it isn't all he gets. Selling her soul is not all there is to life in the underworld. She must appreciate her customer, and be glad of the opportunity to do so. He demands it, expects it, and verifies it by spending his money with those who show him the greatest attention. So all fairies give the "spider and the fly" game to their customers. It does not seem to occur to men THAT IT IS MONEY THAT TALKS with us, and it is NECESSITY THAT MAKES IT TALK.

Vanity of personal appearance in a woman is excusable, but it is unbecoming and despicable in a man.

It often happens that a patron falls desperately in love with one of our girls and insists upon an immediate marriage. If it is congenial to the fairy, the affair takes place and all is well; otherwise SHE KEEPS HIM ON THE STRING, and exchanges "CON" for COIN UNTIL HE IS BADLY BENT, IF NOT BROKE.

We regard this as the proper reception of our patrons, and we all help it along as much

208

Fairy and Victim

as possible. Why should we have mercy for
him? Did men have mercy for us? All we
GET IS HIS MONEY; his reputation,
which he TAKES BACK INTO SOCIE-
TY, IS AS GOOD AS NEW. If men
could but know how we dread them, how we
fear them, and how we HATE MOST OF
THEM, their vanity would disappear.

The man who spends his money freely
with us is known as a PRINCE OF GOOD
FELLOWS, because he spends his money
like a prince.

The good fellow who is a prince is praised,
applauded and humored until he has spent
his last dollar. There are many ways of con-
veying the idea that we believe he is a prince,
and his generosity compels us to be sincere
at times and a pang of remorse is felt at the
part we take in leading him on, but after all
this is waste of sentiment. The man is out
for what he calls a good time, and he thinks
he is getting the worth of his money. Among
ourselves we do not call him "good fellow" or
"prince" but just plain FOOL.

He does not spend his money because of

The Underworld Sewer

any high regard or consideration he has for us, but to gratify his vanity and his recklessness and to enlist our admiration.

Should we from the best of motives have advised him to go home he would not have gone further than the next house, so we bury our good thoughts and proceed to assist him in the experience he is longing for. Hence he is both fleeced and laughed at.

We are obliged to listen to a lot of absurdities from our customers. Some of the chestnuts girls hear regularly, year after year, are as follows: What a lot of pretty girls! It is such a pity that you are in such a place! You would be an ornament to society. Is there no way to quit it? And a long string of such entreaties come to us with regularity. The girls who cannot avoid snickering must leave the room. Such solicitation coming from a man who is on a soul-purchasing trip is so amusing and disgusting that the girls make grimaces when he is not looking.

It is a fashionable by-word the girls use among themselves "IT IS SUCH A PITY THAT YOU ARE IN SUCH A

Fairy and Victim

PLACE," and other expressions which are so frequently repeated by our customers.

The girl in the underworld who can adapt herself to circumstances and is immune to flattery has profited by the experience she has had in her downfall. It is grim necessity with her. She has children or infirm parents depending upon her for support who never know the manner in which she earns her money.

She takes part in the surroundings with energy that is pathetic, by jollying the men along, ridiculing and praising them alternately and drinking wine or beer with them. It seems to be one of the highest ambitions of men to see our girls intoxicated. But she does not seem to be getting drunk! Jupiter! she can stand a lot! The secret is she switches glasses with another girl who presses up against her and in the meantime slips her an empty glass for the full one. Or she WATCHES FOR A CHANCE TO EMPTY IT INTO A CUSPIDOR at her side. MEN LITTLE REALIZE HOW MUCH MONEY THEY SPEND

The Underworld Sewer

TO FILL THIS VESSEL. We have signs and words among ourselves by which we can carry on an understanding without attracting the attention of the customer.

If the girls are not drunk they play drunk to perfection when necessary for a crowd of men who have bought a parlor for a time. The men go away feeling they have put their money to good use and have been well entertained.

THESE MEN HOLD RESPONSIBLE POSITIONS OF ALL KINDS IN THE BUSINESS WORLD and do not seem to regard it as anything out of the way to spend their money for this purpose. Such men are regular customers. THEY DO NOT LOSE THEIR SOCIAL STANDING BY THESE VISITS TO THE UNDERWORLD.

The best class of girls never blackmail. They are not dishonest, are truthful and of high principles. To them it is a business that is loathsome and they are watching a chance to get away from it, and always bearing in mind that the profit they earn GOES TO

Fairy and Victim

SUPPORT THE DEAR ONES AT
HOME AND EVENTUALLY TO RE-
DEEM THEMSELVES. These thoughts
are always uppermost in their minds, al-
though THEIR AMBITIONS ARE
SELDOM REALIZED, AS THERE
IS NO ROOM FOR THEM IN THE
CHRISTIAN WORLD.

The following are questions which have
been asked by our respectable sisters repeat-
edly: "How can the men be carried away by
those ignorant, painted-faced hussies? And
how can we keep our men at home?" I may
be able to answer your interrogations. To
keep your men at home you might try dress-
ing, painting, and wearing decollete dresses
all the time, or red kimonos. RED IS A
FAVORITE SHADE WITH MEN
AND HAS SOME SUCH AN EF-
FECT UPON THEM AS IT HAS
UPON SOME KINDS OF ANIMALS.
Men will pursue a glimpse of anything
red fluttering around the corner in spite of
all. You might try using plenty of red paint
for your face, AND MAKE LOVE TO

The Underworld Sewer

YOUR MEN TO BEAT THE BAND. Show them that they can have ALL OF THAT AT HOME without chasing around the corner for a supply OR PAINTING THE TOWN RED TO OBTAIN THE DESIRED SHADE.

If some of our good ladies were less self-centered it would be observed by them WHERE the fault sometimes lies, and also the power to change it.

You THRIVE AND FEED UPON THE LOVE AND PRAISE which you daily obtain from your men and UNLESS IT COMES WITH REGULARITY THERE IS GRIEVING AND POUTING AND GNASHING OF TEETH, according to the disposition of the dear lady, to whom it does not seem to occur that a man (barring his failings, the size of his body or mind) IS HUMAN and an exact counterpart of yourself in this respect and WITH THE SAME DESIRE FOR LOVE, PRAISE AND APPRECIATION and, FAILING TO OBTAIN IT in his home, he will most likely GO AND BUY IT.

Fairy and Victim

Good men will occasionally resort to the underworld from sheer craving for companionship and appreciation **WHICH HE KNOWS HE MUST PURCHASE TO OBTAIN** and that it is not the genuine "home grown" **BUT A SUBSTITUTE,** concerning which there is a tinge of romance involved **WHICH IS ALLURING AND MOST FATAL.**

CHAPTER XVIII.

The Rich Daughter

The underworld woman is not the only woman who sells herself for a consideration. It is impossible to comprehend the ambition of the millionaire's daughter who chooses in marriage and gives a few millions for a Count, a Lord, a Marquis, or a Duke, who has squandered his immense fortune as well as the fortune of others and who is in debt beyond the financial ability of his royal friends to redeem. The true history of his lineage discloses that his ancestry were not free from all evil associations and conduct.

He is nobility in name only. It does not inspire in the underworld woman a lofty opinion of her rich American sister who pays her millions for an empty title, who brings upon herself, from choice, largely the same condition as the woman who sacrifices herself for money with which to buy bread and cloth-

The Rich Daughter

ing for herself and dependent ones. Both are sold. One secures the title and the other the loaf. From no point can a moral distinction be observed, but it requires greater sacrifice to obtain the loaf than the loafer.

Too little money creates the underworld. Too much money creates fashionable society as it is. Both have a very unwholesome effect upon the balance of the people.

This tribe who have education, who have refinement, who have opportunities, who have wealth, spend most of it in nourishing extreme self indulgence, instead of helping to make the world a better place to live in. So it appears that there are conditions besides the poverty-stricken underworld which should be eradicated.

The rich society lady thinks she deserves a lot of sympathy on account of being a slave to her social obligations. She says "no other position requires the expenditure of so much force and nervous energy." We in the underworld believe that such vital force should be devoted to a better cause than the striving for honor and power which is seldom wholly attained.

The Underworld Sewer

It is a waste of time to feed the glutton who does not observe what you have done. Your best efforts are always more criticized than praised by your own set. But still the striving for distinction continues. Hope whispers to the society woman that JUST OVER THERE you will find all your worldly ambitions realized! The underworld woman has THE SAME DELUSIVE DREAMS WHICH NEVER COME TRUE.

Banquets of every variety and expensive dinners are the result of gross indulgence. The abnormal desire for good things to eat is a cultivated taste just as much as the cravings for drink, only more idiotic if anything, because it just as often requires medical aid to counteract the effect of the good dinner.

The most advanced society strives to outdo each other and will exert its utmost energy to be in the lead, to regale their guests with food to the capacity of their physical natures. It is not to be supposed that banquets and dinners supply their guests with

The Rich Daughter

food of the most hygienic, but that which mostly serves to tickle the palate.

Not all who attend banquets are gluttons, but imagine they are taking a part in the highest and most exalted form of civilized life when the truth is that feasting, eating and drinking and being merry dates back from before the flood.

It is interesting to look forward to the time when a civilized being will study out the food which is most wholesome and adaptable and partake of it in the privacy of their homes for the nourishment of the body instead of utilizing so much time on the manner the food should be conveyed to the mouth or the clothing to be worn to perform this necessary act. Much saving of drudgery for those who must serve would also result. Civilization is a dismal failure if it only means eat, drink and dress to one class and serfdom to the other.

We believe there are dark hours and unhappiness concealed beneath the velvets, laces and diamonds of the rich woman as well as under the laces, diamonds and the glad rags of the underworld woman.

The Underworld Sewer

The great purpose of life is happiness, but the elevated mind is not appeased by what the body can see, hear, taste and handle. The body is the lowest, least important of the components of a human being, and yet we read about million-dollar garments and as we compare such extravagance with what we know and have seen of poverty and crime in all of its nakedness then we agree with the writer who affirms that the church has made a mistake in sending their missionaries to foreign lands while the rich women of our country need their service so much.

The wicked waste of money of the rich does not create the envy which it aims to do. It only calls attention to the shallowness of our leaders, who are supposed to be the highest specimens of womankind according to worldly understanding—WHO DECORATE THEIR BODIES AFTER THE MANNER OF A CHRISTMAS TREE at the same moment THOUSANDS OF PEOPLE WITHIN A SHORT DISTANCE ARE IN A LIFE AND DEATH STRUGGLE FOR EX-

The Rich Daughter

ISTENCE. This does not demonstrate that paganism is a thing of the past.

The evil customs and habits of some of the women who have abundance of wealth are quite similar to women of the underworld —the cigarette smoking, the doping, the drinking and other sins and manifold hypocrisies are very much the same.

Those who wish to know about fashionable society or have ambitions to enter it should first read "A Little Brother of the Rich," by J. M. Patterson.

Considered from a moral standpoint, as the practice is seen by us, it would be no improvement for us to adopt the methods of the reckless women of this set, although they have the respect of the world AND HAVE MANY APES.

The traffic which society makes of marriage is seldom practiced in the underworld, as strange as it may seem. The underworld girl is wholly dominated by love. Greed is not a part of her nature. When marriage is contracted it must be for love alone. She is generally true to her marriage vows which nothing but necessity will change. She is

The Underworld Sewer

compelled to sell her body and soul for food and clothing but her love cannot be bought. In the underworld a Count, a Lord, a Marquis, or a Duke have no more prestige than the most ordinary man. He is a nobleman only if he has the cash for us to purchase necessities.

Where the marital relations are a mere matter of animal instinct or a mere matter of finance, as seems to be the fact in many cases in modern times, what can be the result to progeny except that they mature into degenerates and affinity searchers? The fashionable woman is too much taken up with her social duties to devote much personal attention to her boys. The rich should regard the training of their boys to a higher sense of honor of more importance than training for social duties or even for financial success.

If the millionaire woman would become interested in the all important question of the day, which does not mean self indulgence but the uplifting of humanity, she would gain greater happiness and distinction than any other way.

Commence anywhere and everywhere, it

The Rich Daughter

all has a bearing on the underworld. There are opportunities and necessities in all directions—in your own circle and all along the line—to those who have already been sacrificed publicly to an immoral existence. Devote at least some of your thousands for education and training schools in the slums. And also for protecting the needy young women of our nation against the temptations and pitfalls and intrigue which brings them to the underworld.

By your efforts everything is possible. You could remove mountains of sin with your millions, not by endowing colleges, churches, hospitals and libraries, but by wiping out the slums where the poor are huddled together and where much of the worst crimes and diseases originate.

Occasionally we hear of some rich philanthropist going down in the slums and leaving a crumb, which is a worthy act, as every crumb helps, but it demands persistent work —many crumbs and great energy—to wipe out the evil. Reaching and overcoming the CAUSE of the social evil must be the final work of this generation.

CHAPTER XIX.

The Unwritten Law

Cain was the FIRST BORN of Adam and Eve. He was also the FIRST MURDERER, for which the Lord condemned him. Since then murder has been known as the most hideous of all crimes.

In modern times it is not murder to kill your antagonist in self defense. It is not murder for you to kill a hungry man who is entering your house through the window in the night time with intention to steal a loaf of bread which he sees lying on the dining room table. Such killing is justifiable homicide. When a burglar breaks into your house to steal your diamonds or money you may use your gun and you are considered a brave man.

But if a villain breaks into a family circle and by intrigue and strategy makes love to and steals the most precious jewel, the repu-

224

The Unwritten Law

tation of a wife or daughter, in such case the husband or father who kills the villain is a murderer under the law and must be put in jail, refused bail, and prosecuted, be tried by a jury for a heinous crime and, according to the law, must be found guilty of murder and put to death or serve a term in the penitentiary. Such killing can not be justified under the law.

However, if there is enough money, influence or sentiment with the father, mother or husband who does the killing, to gain public notice and commendation and fee good lawyers the accused may put up a spiel that when the act was committed he or she was insane.

The jury consisting of twelve HONEST men, who are selected and sworn to try the case and render a verdict according to the law and evidence, and to not permit sympathy or prejudice to have any weight in arriving at a decision.

The judge upon the bench is under solemn oath to be governed by the constitution and laws of the land and uphold the dig-

The Underworld Sewer

nity thereof. The bailiff in charge of the jury is sworn to keep the jurors free from all outside influence and not allow them to read any newspapers commenting on the case during the trial, or talk about the case. The jury is daily cautioned and sworn to not permit any one to talk in their presence about the case and to not read any items in print relating to it. The lawyers are under oath to support and maintain the constitution and laws at all times and under all circumstances.

The trial begins under the most solemn conditions. The killing is proved not only beyond a reasonable doubt, but positive, and beyond dispute. No incident is disclosed tending to show that the defendants did not proceed to the act of killing in the most natural and practical way known to humanity and a clear case of murder in the first degree is established.

Then counsel for the defendant proceeds to show that the great-grandfather of defendant had peculiarities of his own and had been accused of being a little off in the upper story when he was elected to Congress. Then

The Unwritten Law

some of the near relations are shown up to have had traits of insanity mixed in their history and finally the life history of the defendant discloses that he had acted in a strange manner many times, and especially a short time before he did the killing, and more especially after he learned what the villain had accomplished.

The doctors have examined him with great care and are quite certain that he was insane, while other doctors are quite positive that he was absolutely sane. The lawyers divide upon that question according to their respective sides.

The court instructs the jury that it must not be swayed by sympathy or prejudice and if the jury shall find that at the time the prisoner did the killing the prisoner was insane the jury shall find the defendant not guilty.

The lawyer for the prisoner is greatly honored for his ability to manufacture testimony to free the prisoner. The witnesses are excused for giving MADE-UP testimony; the jury is praised for accepting it; the ver-

The Underworld Sewer

dict is based on the insanity of the prisoner,
which everybody knows is not true, and the
judge commends the jury for their most ex-
cellent service.

Such a case is governed by what is known
as the "unwritten law." When you say that
the prisoner has escaped the gallows by virtue of the "unwritten law" you mean that
according to the written constitution and
law, and the truth, the prisoner was guilty
of murder and for the occasion all law has
been cast aside by reason of the influence,
money and public sentiment.

If this unwritten law would secure a verdict of NOT GUILTY for a poor man who
cannot pay the expense of putting up the insanity defense and proving himself insane,
it would have the good effect of preventing
many ruffians from bringing ruin to the reputation of women through fear of the consequences.

As a practical proposition, the unwritten
law benefits the rich only.

If the law should be written that the
injured husband father, mother, brother

The Unwritten Law

might slay the man who robs the daughter, sister or wife of her reputation there would be a sudden increase of male funerals and also a corresponding decrease in the number of ruined reputations of girls and women.

I would not advocate the taking of human life under any circumstances, nothing can make it justifiable.

But these real conditions illustrate the inconsistency of human laws and civilized customs.

It is lawful to kill a man who enters your window to steal bread; it is murder to kill a man who destroys the reputation of your daughter.

Within a few years there have been several murders in succession in high life, which came under the head of the unwritten law, and were tried under the insanity plea.

Those of the most recent and well known cases are Stanford White, who was shot and killed by Harry K. Thaw for ravishing his wife. Also, Judge Loving of West Virginia, who killed Theodore Estes for the same offence, involving his daughter.

The Underworld Sewer

And again, Mrs. Bradley, who sent to the happy hunting ground the senatorial Indian, Brown, and the father of her children, who refused to consummate the square deal which he had promised her for many years.

Evelyn Thaw has given a description of her experience in open court, in language so plain as not to be mistaken in its meaning, many people regarded it as nauseating and refused to read, much less believe it.

But we in the underworld can verify her in all she has said, we know it to be absolutely true, every word of it. WE RECOGNIZE IT AS AN OLD STORY, well known to the girls in the underworld, a story WHICH HAS NOT, EVEN HALF OF IT, EVER BEEN TOLD.

In fact, the underworld is full of victims of similar experience, of which the rich vultures have been the offender. It is a common occurrence for rich men to be guilty of this specie of iniquity in which these men indulged, and some of our men who are posing as honored citizens in our land would plead guilty if they would dare admit the truth.

The Unwritten Law

It would be difficult to guess what a man or woman would do under such circumstances, as the experience of Thaw, Loving and Mrs. Bradley.

Certain it is that the world is better without men who leave devastation and ruin in their path wherever they go.

There is no punishment too severe for the ravisher. He commits a crime that the brute creation condemns.

The laws of the land should be made so severe in the protection of a woman's reputation that a man would scarcely take the risk of the penalty.

Is there very much difference in the real crime, whether a woman is overcome by violence, deceit, drugs or hypnotic influence?

Murder is not of frequent occurrence in the underworld. Has it been observed?— But our suicides are many.

More recently our county has witnessed a series of such crimes, committed by imitators, and ALL MORE OR LESS PROMINENT IN SOCIETY.

The man who is vindicated by the unwrit-

The Underworld Sewer

ten law, after having shot the villain down who has invaded his home, does not deserve the maudlin sympathy with which he is swamped.

As a matter of fact, in ninety-nine cases out of a hundred, when an outraged husband cries out against offended honor HE HAS HIMSELF BROUGHT THE CONDITION ABOUT, while his own home has been violated, created chiefly by misdeeds of his own too numerous to mention, he has been ENGAGED IN THE SAME KIND OF INTRIGUE WITH ANOTHER MAN'S WIFE; or is SPENDING HIS TIME AND MONEY IN THE UNDERWORLD. The unwritten law is the means through which the natural born coward, the bully, the renegade and the fool goes to gratify his vindictiveness, he is perpetually on the lookout for the wrecker of his home, while his own life has long been as black as Hades, out of which he emerges rampant to vent his wrath upon a defenseless man, BELIEVING THE JURY WILL ACQUIT HIM OF THE CRIME.

The Unwritten Law

Here the sympathy belongs to the woman, although she may have been involved in a dubious position, in most cases the husband set the example.

It has been woman's custom since the world began to be the first to condemn her own sex. She, who has always remained upon the high pedestal, having had no temptation to come down—instead of stooping to lift—heaps vituperations upon her who has departed from the straight path. WHY IS THIS?

If the real object of a certain captain had been to save his home and to keep the disgrace from his children, he could have done so. But he chose to be the assassin, and to put the finishing touches of infamy to his own home, as well as to the home of his supposed foe, knowing he could do so with impunity.

The sacredness of the home is what a man makes it; he is the axle on which everything hinges; on him depends the smooth running or the clogging of the wheels. The good man who lives a pure, clean life is idol-

The Underworld Sewer

ized in his home; there is no room for a serpent to creep in.

In a land where there are pyramids of jurisprudence touching upon all questions, and where everybody is confronted by a code of some sort wherever they turn, it would seem that the unwritten law might be fathomed and written that a limitation may be put upon it.

A law enacted to cover the unwritten one would be no more formidable than to RE-QUIRE THE ONE WHO FIRES THE FATAL SHOT TO BE MORALLY PURE AND OTHERWISE FLAWLESS, or be sentenced to life imprisonment. This would debar the men from taking the law in their hands, and also some of the women; the balance would be too spotless, wise and civilized to commit a crime for vengeance. However, while the unwritten law exists, the privilege to use it SHOULD BE CONFERRED TO WOMEN ONLY.

CHAPTER XX.

Parents

Do you say it is dangerous or improper to talk upon this subject of social evil with your family?

Do you say that it is degrading for good people to do any thinking upon this subject?

Do you believe it best that you should keep the whole subject a profound secret from your family circle and leave it for boys and girls to learn of it in the street or from those who are leading the wrong way?

Do you believe that your girls and boys will grow up to be men and women without ever hearing of this monster evil?

Do you believe that you can so train your boys and girls, with this evil in your city, so that they will not imbibe any information upon the subject, that may be given them gratuitously by associates?

Would it not be better to ABOLISH

235

The Underworld Sewer

THE SYSTEM which has for MANY CENTURIES TRIED TO KEEP the secret of the UNDERWORLD SEWER away from the children, WITHOUT SUCCESS?

Every decent human being wants the re-regard above all of his children, and they will also anxiously guard them lest the truth of the evil be known. But in a brief space of time they are bound to know of the skeleton in the closet.

Each of you remembers the first inkling of vice which reached your ear during your childhood days; how eager you were to learn more, how you never lost an opportunity to unravel the mystery.

The children are aware of the fact that there are secrets being kept from them, and when they are "BIG ENOUGH TO KNOW" that many things will be revealed to them.

Your own children are the exact copy of your mother's children in this respect, also your grandparents' children.

Away back—the long line of ancestors—

Parents

all children have been curiously on the alert to LEARN THE SECRET WHICH IS BEING KEPT FROM THEM.

YOU, who are THE FATHERS OF FAMILIES, have voted to keep the underworld and the saloon for the business, and the money it puts in circulation, as necessary evils; like your own parents, YOU are trying to KEEP ALL INFORMATION relating to the social evil AWAY FROM YOUR CHILDREN, but you will have no more success in HIDING THE REAL CONDITION FROM YOUR CHILDREN than YOUR PARENTS HAD IN HIDING the secret from THEIR CHILDREN.

It can't be kept from the children long. When it is known to them, they are more than likely to make some investigations of their own, in the same manner that you did when a child, and have continued so doing since you have become a man.

It WOULD GRIEVE YOU BEYOND MEASURE to know that your CHILDREN WOULD EVER KNOW

The Underworld Sewer

AS MUCH ABOUT THE EVIL AS YOU DO; your own parents had the same anxiety. AND THUS IT WILL CONTINUE UNTIL THE EVIL CEASES TO BE REGARDED AS A NECESSITY.

Your anxiety should be with your grown up children. Train your boys as carefully as you will, when they grow up they will find the underworld, as long as it exists.

Abolish the saloon and the underworld, the evils you are ashamed of, and there will be no secrets TO KEEP from the children. When the young man starts out to see THE ELEPHANT he is not prepared for the consequences he will encounter.

The public and private schools are teaching the students that the use of tobacco and intoxicating drinks are poisonous to the system. The students are urged to refrain from their use. But there has yet been NO WAY FOUND OR ATTEMPTED TO CAUTION THE YOUNG PEOPLE OF THE DANGER, DISGRACE, SICKNESS AND DISEASE WHICH FOL-

Parents

LOW IN THE WAKE OF IMMO-
RALITY.

The day must come, and IT OUGHT TO
ARRIVE SOON, when the social evil and
its dangers will be discussed in the family
more freely, without any thought of vulgar-
ity or impropriety.

If you MUST have the evil, talk it over
with your family, and put them on their
guard, rather than have them learn it from
other sources.

Explain to them that yonder lies the great
underworld; it is a sewer, through which to
DRAIN ALL MORAL IMPURITIES
FROM THE CHRISTIAN WORLD,
but the existence of this sewer IS JUST
AS NECESSARY AS ANY OTHER
SEWER. THE WOMEN WHOSE
MISSION IT IS TO BE CONSIGNED
THERE ARE SINNERS, AND THE
WAGES OF SIN IS DEATH. IT IS
A PLACE WHERE DISCORD AND
DARKNESS PERVADE EVERY-
THING. IT IS THE ABIDING
PLACE OF ALL FOUL THINGS

The Underworld Sewer

THAT A PERVERTED IMAGINA-
TION CAN CONCEIVE, AND AN
EXISTENCE FROM WHICH NO
ONE RETURNETH. Tell them that
they have the very FIERCEST ANIMAL
DOWN THERE, it is called conditions,
and IT IS FIERCE; THEY HAVE
PROVIDED A CAGE FOR IT, BUT
NO CAGE IS STRONG ENOUGH TO
HOLD IT. THE ONLY WAY IS TO
SHUN IT, because it brings destruction
and death everlasting.

Hearing of the evil from others causes a
child to use artful means of evasion to prevent the parent from knowing that he is in
possession of the secret. Do you remember
how terribly innocent you appeared, WHEN
YOU KNEW A WHOLE LOT ALL
THE TIME? Although you were merely
a child YOU WERE ASHAMED OF
WHAT YOU KNEW; you were aware
that all of the BIG FOLKS WERE
ASHAMED OF SOMETHING TOO.
You have an idea that your children are not
so prying; YOUR OWN PARENTS
HAD THE SAME IDEA.

Parents

PARENT, of course you are ashamed of this animal, AND YOU OUGHT TO BE. It is your duty to dispatch him and give your children the training and education that will best fit them when they grow to be men and women, to realize that the greatest obstacle to progression is the saloon and the underworld evils.

There are some instructions that do not come in the line of the church or school, and sometimes the parents are not qualified to furnish them. To obviate this IT WOULD SEEM THAT THERE SHOULD BE CLUBS INAUGURATED EVERYWHERE TO BRING THE MOTHERS OF DIFFERENT CLASSES TOGETHER; the "National Congress of Mothers for the Welfare of the Child" is one of the GREATEST MOVEMENTS FOR HIGHER IDEALS of modern times, and if the teachings promulgated by these good ladies can REACH THE HUMBLEST MOTHER with the big family, and THE YOUNG MOTHER, it will be a move that will tend to revolutionize things.

241

The Underworld Sewer

What does the average young couple know about raising children? They are expected to know how to do this without any instruction.

The young couple love their children, to be sure, and provide them with food and clothing according to their means. And sometimes they try to teach them "manners," which is a worthy beginning, but manners aren't morals, any more than sour krout is apple sauce.

Manners deal with outward polish, while morality is a state that holds itself aloof from impurity of mind and body. Justice is the honest and conscientious treatment dealt out to a friend or a fellow being.

Although it has been refuted, the individual who is guided by conscience will not fall very short of doing the right thing at all times. I believe that conscientiousness should be developed to the highest degree.

And he or she who disobeys the dictates of the conscience WILL SUFFER AC-CORDINGLY.

If it was developed, he or she WOULD

Parents

BE WILLING TO CEASE WRONG-DOING IN ORDER TO AVOID THE SELF-ADMINISTERED punishment it would bring.

The most relentless judge is CONSCIENCE, and the most severe punishment is REMORSE.

CHAPTER XXI

Reform Schools

Our reform or industrial schools for girls are failures in many respects.

In the first place, the girls regard it a most terrible disgrace to be so publicly exposed, and the sentence follows them as long as their identity can be traced.

To them it does not imply reform, but only persecution and imprisonment.

A boy may go to a reform school, and come out and follow any avocation, and can be proud of his record in the school, and he is a man among men, and rather honored for having come out all right, and not disgraced.

But with a girl it is different; if she has been sent there on account of some man, who does not have to blush for the shame he has brought upon her, yet there is her record.

Reform Schools

The many girls I have met in the underworld who have had a siege of the reform school have the same complaints to make, which are that the evil, unknown to them before they arrived at the school, they learned from each other while at school, and they became wiser in the way of vice than when they entered.

Girls who are persuaded into wrongdoing through the influence of others are not criminals, and they should not be treated as such.

It is the greatest mistake that can be made to suppose that girls are guilty of all kinds of crime because they have fallen from grace.

When they return to their homes from the school, they are not the same in the estimation of their friends.

They can not get away from their record. They are frowned upon and cut by their friends. Young men and girls of their acquaintance do not dare make companions of them.

There is no surer way of driving a young girl to the underworld than to send her to a

The Underworld Sewer

reformatory, unless her identity, or the cause of detention, can be covered up.

I have known girls with many good traits of character to come to the underworld from the reform schools so filled with resentment, wrath and censure against their parents or guardians who were instrumental in sending them to the reform school, and forever disgracing them with their friends, the effect of which was that when the first opportunity afforded they came to the underworld.

It reflects upon the judgment and wisdom of the parents or guardians to send their girls to the reform school. There is something wrong in the management and the home influence, and ignorance of the parents who might themselves improve by a term in some reformatory.

CHAPTER XXII.

Club Women

What are the different club women doing toward relieving the distress of the fallen women? Anything besides instigating a punishment for them?

I do not hear of any special effort that the Woman's Christian Temperance Union are making in our behalf.

In all kindness, I must say to the ladies of the club and church, which constitutes the most elevated society, that THERE ARE MANY GIRLS IN THE UNDER-WORLD WHO HAVE BEEN EM-PLOYED BY YOU IN SOME CA-PACITY, WHO HAVE NO FLAT-TERING REPORT TO DETAIL re-garding your consideration for them. IN EVERY INSTANCE I believe all THESE GIRLS COULD HAVE BEEN SAVED had you regarded it as

The Underworld Sewer

WORTH WHILE TO TAKE ANY INTEREST IN THEM when in your employment.

The very name of "Young Women's Christian Association" would suggest that all members are taught and required that they must do Christian acts.

If such is not the intention, the name should be changed to *home for pious young women.*

IF A YOUNG GIRL FROM THE UNDERWORLD WERE TO APPLY TO THEM FOR SHELTER, with the intention of DISCONTINUING HER SINFUL LIFE, WOULD THESE YOUNG LADIES of the Christian Association BEFRIEND THIS WRETCHED HUMAN BEING? NOT AT ALL; but on the contrary, SHE WOULD BE REGARDED AS *"having her nerve"* AND QUICKLY SENT AWAY. SHE WOULD NOT BE TOLERATED A MINUTE.

Is it enough that these young ladies say their prayers regularly and are living moral lives in a pure atmosphere?

248

Club Women

Why should the girl who is endeavoring to reform be LEFT ENTIRELY TO PROFESSIONAL REFORMERS?

IT SHOULD BE the BUSINESS of EVERY CHRISTIAN woman to lend a helping hand.

THE COMBINED EFFORT of all to PREVENT THE INFLUX TO THIS VORTEX OF MISERY is a gigantic undertaking, but the only means to accomplish results is FOR ALL TO WORK IN HARMONY TO THIS END.

The ladies should guard against not being the conscious or unconscious cause of discouraging the girls, and helping to send them to the underworld. IT IS TIME THAT YOU SHOULD DEFEND YOUR OWN SEX.

The act of snubbing the unfortunate women on every occasion SHOULD BECOME UNFASHIONABLE.

Our girls would rather remain in their own vile state all their lives than to be REMINDED CONSTANTLY OF THEIR SINS WITH SUCH VENOM.

The Underworld Sewer

"Two wrongs don't make a right," has been demonstrated long ago. THE DE-SIRE TO REFORM IS NOT EN-COURAGED BY SNEERS AND SCORNFUL ATTACKS.

A kind word spoken to one of us, a look of sympathy bestowed upon one of us, an act of kindness toward one of us, or a sentence which shows that there IS A BRIGHTER SIDE TO LIFE; SUCH INTEREST EXPRESSED BY A WOMAN WHOSE SOUL HAS NOT BEEN TARNISHED, ARE MES-SAGES OF LOVE THAT ARE RE-PEATED AGAIN AND AGAIN to associates in the underworld.

And does more toward reforming our girls than all the punishment meted out to us, and all the prayers offered up in our favor from the pulpit and the pews.

We have a high regard for a respectable woman, and if she chances to meet us, and would treat us with such consideration, SHE WOULD BE CHERISHED as a GUARDIAN ANGEL, and in OUR

Club Women

TRIALS AND SORROWS, that kind
ACT WOULD REMAIN as a GUID-
ING STAR.

Such is the understanding of real Christianity by the underworld woman; and no
other can have any effect upon her.

The professional way of reforming is a
mighty cold-blooded affair.

CHAPTER XXIII.

Plain Talks

Many club and society women, who are Christians and real ladies, too, enjoy repeating the smutty stories and jokes which they have heard from their husbands.

These stories are told when they meet in small impromptu groups and men are not present.

On a certain occasion a woman from the underworld was present incognito, and knowing that she was in the company of highly respected and refined women, she was expecting a treat of culture and refinement, and as the evening progressed found much to encourage her in her resolution to make a complete reformation.

However, later in the evening one of the ladies offered to tell a story that she had heard from her husband the day before.

Plain Talks

They all listened and laughed. Although the stories bordered strong on smut, one after another of these stories were told by the different ladies, to attentive ears and followed by hearty laughter and very commonplace comments.

The woman from the underworld was not only surprised, BUT SHOCKED, at the repetition of these coarse and vulgar stories, in this refined and Christian society; and the more shocked to see that the whole crowd enjoyed the most vulgar stories best.

The stories were identically the same as the underworld woman had heard told by men visitors in her own parlors.

It wasn't the stories which shocked the woman, but THE SOURCE FROM WHICH THEY CAME.

When the society women go slumming in the underworld they will find what they are looking for. But the underworld woman goes slumming in society, and is disgusted with what she finds.

The underworld woman went back to her business feeling that IF SHE MUST

The Underworld Sewer

HEAR ODIOUS LANGUAGE, SHE
MAY AS WELL REMAIN WHERE
THE UNEXPECTED NEVER HAP-
PENS.

You may regard the story-telling as a little deviltry, as having no significance except
to amuse you for a few moments; there is no
EXCUSE FOR A RESPECTABLE
WOMAN TO TELL A SMUTTY
STORY, or permit one to be told to her,
either by a husband or a lady friend.

Smut talking among the ladies, when a
few are gathered together, is a common occurrence.

"For out of the abundance of the heart
his mouth speaketh," and "for it is a shame
even to speak of those things which are done
of them in secret."—Eph. v:12.

Society can not escape the criticism of the
underworld any more than the underworld
can escape the criticism of society.

NUMBER 2.

It has been said, and is generally so understood, that foundlings' homes and child

Plain Talks

saving institutes are full of children from the underworld.

Such is not the fact. It is true, however, that women who leave their children with such homes often come to the underworld.

There are very few children born in the underworld; the life the women lead is in violation of the laws of nature.

The Creator seems to have decreed that nature should cease unfolding and reproduction terminate where it has been so offended as it is in the underworld.

Maternity is too sacred an obligation to happen often here.

The few children which are born are sent to private homes and cared for by the mothers, and are seldom offered for adoption.

They never commit the crime of murdering their offspring before birth, which is a common occurrence in the Christian world; this crime is reserved for the respectable Christian woman.

The few children that are born in the underworld are, I repeat, NEVER destroyed. I can hear my Christian sisters say: "It would be better if they were."

The Underworld Sewer

This suggestion is contrary to the religion you follow, and makes us feel that we do not want any of such Christianity.

In our circle it is considered that the most honorable thing to do is to support and keep our child in a respectable home and give it an education—and at the same time keep it in ignorance of our business.

There is nothing that justifies murder. It is just as much murder to destroy the child before it is born as afterward. Although the doctors claim that such is not the fact, but they have reasons of their own for expressing such an opinion.

Whether a woman has a good home, a poor home or no home at all, or whether she is rich or poor, is no excuse for her to commit this crime.

In the near future it will be discovered that even marriage does not confer all kinds of license. The remedy for your trouble is a platonic life.

NUMBER 3.

It would seem that in this day of advancement, men employed on the police force

Plain Talks

would be chosen from the educated class, because it is a position which calls for the exercise of judgment and discrimination in the highest degree at all times. A police officer comes in contact with the evil as it really exists, and has at all times a chance to be humane, and also great opportunity to apply remedies other than jailing, WHICH SHOULD ALWAYS be the LAST RESORT, AS IT DON'T BENEFIT THE DEGRADED GIRL, and it DEGRADES THE ONE WITH AMBITIONS TO FREE HERSELF FROM THE LIFE.

When an ignorant man is invested with authority, his domineering, bullying and injustice knows no bounds.

We are at the mercy of the police, who are as a rule treacherous, mean, familiar and offensive in their manners.

It is well known that we are sometimes blackmailed by them, but it is not always money they demand.

THEY ASSUME AN AIR OF OWNERSHIP OF US, BODY AND

The Underworld Sewer

SOUL, and if WE CROSS THEM IN ANY WAY, they will ARREST US ON THE SPOT.

Or they will make US FEEL THAT IT IS BY REASON OF THEIR CHARITY AND INFLUENCE WE ARE ALLOWED TO REMAIN UNDISTURBED.

They pretend to be friendly, when at the same time they are watching for an excuse to arrest us. If a girl has heedlessly permitted an officer to learn that she has been SOMEWHAT LUCKY IN MONEY GETTING, and the officer has been particularly friendly, he PRETENDS TO HAVE BUSINESS ELSEWHERE while the arrest is being made, in order that he MAY KEEP HER CONFIDENCE and repeat the trick.

Money grabbing is visible everywhere in the underworld; WE ARE BRUSHED ASIDE AS THAT MANY FLIES, OR ROUNDED UP AS THAT MANY CATTLE on the slightest provocation. The impression is that WE "MAKE OUR

Plain Talks

MONEY EASY." We must submit lamb-like to ANY CONDITIONS THE PO-LICE SEE FIT TO MAKE FOR US; we can't help ourselves, we should be THANKFUL that we are ALLOWED TO LIVE AT ALL, seems to be the inference of the police.

It is the INEXPERIENCED GIRLS in the SMALLER HOUSES who are MOSTLY IMPOSED UPON in this respect, and more especially THOSE WHO ARE NOT IN PUBLIC HOUSES, but LIVING IN ROOMS HERE AND THERE; they are THROWN IN JAIL on the STRENGTH OF A SUSPICION, AND MADE TO GO INTO ONE OF THESE PUBLIC ESTABLISH-MENTS. MANY OF THESE GIRLS would otherwise never REACH THE UNDERWORLD.

The BRUTAL TREATMENT we receive from the police officer HE CALLS "DISCIPLINE," when it is NOTHING more than TERRORIZING AND A DE-

The Underworld Sewer

SIRE TO CALL ATTENTION to his own importance, and INCREASE HIS MERIT MARKS IN THE DEPARTMENT. True discipline can only come from a clear conception of justice, A SENSE WHICH THE OFFICER SELDOM POSSESSES.

For a TRIVIAL BLUNDER a girl is arrested. To attempt to make an explanation is termed "talking back" and "sassing"; for this offense she can not escape a fine. INDIGNITIES AND HUMILIATIONS of every nature we must endure, IN SILENCE, from the man who is representing the law. The underworld woman would have great reverence for the proper man, BUT NOT WHEN THE MAN'S PRINCIPLES ARE BELOW HER OWN STANDARD.

The more ignorant the officer, the more he will presume upon his authority. THE FEW EXCEPTIONS are those who are gentlemanly and considerate, WITHOUT REWARD OF ANY KIND; THEY HAVE NO IDEA HOW MUCH

Plain Talks

HOPE AND ENCOURAGEMENT THEY INSPIRE IN US.

NUMBER 4.

Church hospitals are so prejudiced against us that we can not obtain proper care therein, even though we pay liberally for service.

These institutions do not contribute much solace to the girl when it is known that she is from the underworld.

One would think that THE TENDEREST CARE WOULD BE GIVEN THIS HOMELESS, MOTHERLESS CREATURE OF THE SEWER, but you are wasting your good thoughts.

This girl may call again and again for assistance WITHOUT RECEIVING A REPLY; FOOD OR ANYTHING IS PUSHED OR FLUNG AT THE PATIENT. It is with a SCOWL that NEVER LEAVES the FACE OF THE ATTENDANT, that she waits upon the underworld girl.

Our women have absolutely no friends outside of their own world; no flood of pity

261

The Underworld Sewer

will rush into the souls of good people for our benefit.

Wherever WE ARE KNOWN WE ARE OVERCHARGED AND PLUNDERED; stores and business houses of all kinds solicit our patronage, and every attention is showered upon us so long as we are in their establishments spending our money, WHICH IS NEVER TOO TAINTED TO BE IN DEMAND.

But these people with whom we deal do not so much as TURN THEIR HEADS IN OUR DIRECTION WHEN THEY MEET US UPON THE STREET.

When they come to the sewer to spend their money, they are friendly with us, but WE DARE NOT BY EITHER WORD OR LOOK RECOGNIZE OUR MOST INTIMATE ACQUAINTANCE, in the open.

In all cities, large or small, this is a noticeable treatment for the inhabitants of the proscribed district.

Do you think that the underworld women have no pride and are destitute of all feeling?

Plain Talks

Do you think that when the policemen add insult to injury that it does not hurt her?

Do you think that when the people of her acquaintance pass her by unnoticed that she feels no pang of pain?

Do you think that when the Sisters who are following in the footsteps of our Savior refuse to give the fallen woman the care which she is paying for, because she is a sinner, that she does not feel grieved and hurt over this treatment?

A fallen woman has the same feelings that others have, there is no difference.

She will always remain a woman, and is conscious of all the injury and injustice heaped upon her.

If you have an idea that there is one woman in one thousand who REMAINS IN THE BUSINESS AS A MATTER OF CHOICE, IN THE NAME OF HUMANITY ALLOW YOURSELF TO BE SHOWN THAT YOU ARE MISTAKEN.

I repeat the assertion that there is not ONE IN A THOUSAND, except the

OUR SUICIDES ARE MANY

The Underworld Sewer

dope fiend, the drunkard or the imbecile, who do not daily wish and PLAN FOR A DELIVERANCE FROM THE LIFE.

We remember our homes where PEACE, PURITY AND LOVE REIGNED, we LONG FOR IT, but PUBLIC SENTIMENT and conditions put us in the underworld forever.

Your opinion makes us an OUTCAST, a BEGGAR, and a SLAVE. All nature speaks to us of love and peace; the animal kingdom respect us as it respects you.

In fact, all of God's creatures are our FRIENDS, except the GOOD MEN AND WOMEN.

We attempt to retain our self-respect, the only trait that may be used as a stepping-stone to redemption.

When pride and hope cease to be a domineering feature of the underworld woman she commits suicide.

Marvel not that so many take this step; BUT RATHER MARVEL THAT MANY MORE DO NOT GO THAT WAY.

Plain Talks

There is a HUMANE LAW prohibiting the abuse of DOGS, but there is NO SUCH PROTECTION for our girls.

My good Christian sisters, I know what your sentiment is on this subject. You will say the fallen woman has forfeited all claim to the consideration to which she thinks she is entitled.

You will say that the life which she is leading PLACES HER BENEATH YOUR NOTICE.

You will say that she must be kept in obscure places, where she can not flaunt her BRAZEN DEEDS in the face of respectability.

You will say that the police must KEEP HER SUBDUED and under control.

You will say the church hospitals must not be filled with these girls anyway.

You will say that a fallen woman is a degenerate, and unless she reforms according to your particular plan of salvation, she SHOULD BE PUNISHED AND DRIVEN AWAY.

You say she is bold and lazy; that she leads the men and boys astray.

The Underworld Sewer

You say that she does not want to reform.

You say there are churches, there are reformatories, there are Open Doors and Rescue Homes, and there are reformers and preachers to assist the fallen women in every manner.

Therefore you conclude there is NOTHING THAT YOU CAN DO TO HELP THE FALLEN WOMAN.

My Christian sister, the church preachers and reformers do not offer us a permanent place nor suggest means to supply ourselves with food, clothing and home, and we have never received any such protection from you; ALL THAT YOU HAVE TO OFFER IS MERELY TEMPORARY.

My Christian sisters, have you nothing to offer but your religion? Suppose that we offered to do our best to obtain your religion and practice it as you practice it, would you be willing to find us employment whereby we can be fed, housed and clothed in an independent, respectable way?

And will you permit us to associate with your sons, daughters and husbands?

Plain Talks

IS YOUR HOME OPEN TO US UPON SUCH CONDITIONS?

Is your home open to us upon any fair basis, EITHER FROM A BUSINESS OR SOCIAL STANDPOINT?

Can we reform without the provision for FOOD, CLOTHING AND RESPECTABILITY?

If not, HOW CAN THIS PROVISION BE MADE? That is the question.

CHAPTER XXIV.

Nature

Human nature is the creature of the senses, the mind, the intellect.

The faculties are driven by the will power as the steam drives the engine.

The professor who asserts that human nature cannot change encourages the selfish, coarse and immoral man, who believes with the professor that he is compelled by propensities in the nature which is impossible to change.

The truth is when there is a real desire, or an opportunity, the change is made, for better or for worse, according to the environments of the individual.

Each individual does his or her part in regenerating human nature, and every good act, word or thought tends towards the evolution.

While the improvements must begin

Nature

in ourselves, the CONDITION SUR-
ROUNDING OURSELVES MUST BE
SUCH AS TO MAKE the beginning pos-
sible.

Our natures are MOLDED BY EN-
VIRONMENTS, the character of which
generates the will power, which determines
the destiny of the individual.

Man has accomplished great things in har-
nessing the vegetable, mineral and animal
kingdom. The master mind of man, with
all of its selfishness, has brought the world
to its present stage. It will be the higher
development of that same mind which continues to improve it.

We have only to look backward to be convinced that human nature must first be improved before it can make improvements,
and that its capacity is almost limitless. If
an individual would resolve to put his own
nature in harness with the same amount of
energy and determination with which he has,
and is controlling exterior elements, and
making scientific researches he would make
rapid strides ethically. Nature's big field

The Underworld Sewer

can not be cultivated in spots with success. The ultimate destiny of the human race is PERFECTION, the greatest obstruction to this end is immorality.

Those who LIVE FOR SELF-IN-DULGENCE rob life of its purpose, and EVENTUALLY LEAVE IT ON A BARREN ROCK, or in the SEWER.

The intellect should control the senses.

Nature without moral training repre-sents the lower propensities of mankind. It is OBSERVABLE THAT THIS TRAINING HAS OFTEN BEEN OMITTED FROM THE EDUCA-TION OF MEN OF THE HIGHEST CULTURE.

If the master mind of the world, in the past, had searched as faithfully for the im-provements from a moral standpoint as they have from the scientific point of view, human nature would now be far above its present standard.

CHAPTER XXV.

The Clergy

From the underworld we see the pulpit from three different views, the broad scholarly mind who is aware that an evil of such magnitude as the social evil has its SOURCE, and that the inhabitants of the underworld ARE THE CHILDREN OF THAT SOURCE. He instructs his hearers that it is to this SOURCE OF SUPPLY THAT THE REMEDY MUST BE APPLIED.

Then there is the fashionable preacher who does not concern himself in the saving of souls outside of his own church.

The most numerous, and also the MOST FAMILIAR TO US IS THE POLITICAL PREACHER, WHO HELPS TO DRIVE US FROM PILLAR TO POST in his ardent desire to redeem us. About the time of city election the underworld expects the regular program to be carried out.

271

The Underworld Sewer

The politician is in search of votes, and there is no better method to get them coming his way then to interest the minister in his behalf.

During the past year these preachers have been particularly active against us.

There is no doubt of the good intention of the preacher, but it is to be REGRETTED THAT SUCH GOOD INTENTIONS, GOOD LABOR, GOOD ENERGY should be usurped by the politician to further his ambition, AS HE ALONE REAPS THE BENEFIT.

The political preacher is largely guided by enthusiasm, the office seeker knows how to keep this characteristic aroused to a certain pitch that he may depend upon him for support during the campaign. The presence and influence of the preacher lends seriousness to the campaign that is of inestimable value to the candidate.

The sharp politician will sometimes go the rounds of the churches and patronize the contribution box very liberally and in such a manner that the minister shall hear the

The Clergy

eagles scream. The minister takes this friendliness to mean that the candidate, with proper treatment, will do a great deal for the Lord, and be a mighty good officer.

The candidate gives the minister pointers as to what must be done to drive all the underworld women out of the city.

Stirred up to the highest pitch, with ambitions of different varieties, the candidate and the minister jumps into the underworld with BOTH FEET and SCATTER THE INHABITANTS RIGHT AND LEFT.

It is not generally known or observed that the minister who preaches the gospel aids in making hardship and misery for us by helping to throw us into jail or driving us in all directions, WHERE WE HAVE NO PLACE TO LAY OUR HEADS. Each of such attacks degrade us that much more.

We believe that the church and politics should unite in helping the women to escape from their environments, but this cannot be accomplished by the abuse and hardship which the present political preacher seems to think is necessary.

The Underworld Sewer

We have only to refer you to the horrible suffering that was occasioned by the Rev. Parkhurst's frenzied crusade against the underworld evil in New York city in 1901-02, to prove that it is a failure.

In every instance these coarse attempts at reform has brought intense suffering, from which no one but the politician derives any benefit.

These spasmodic waves of morality, which the office seeker turns to selfishness, can have no possible effect upon our condition, and only tends to embitter us.

It would be a hopeless case for the preacher to undertake to redeem the underworld alone; but HE CAN DO MUCH TOWARD PREVENTING GIRLS AND WOMEN FROM GOING THERE.

There must be reasons for the steady influx into this life. Notwithstanding all of the schools, churches, reformers, and preachers, the UNDERWORLD IS FILLED EVERY YEAR TO OVERFLOW.

"An ounce of precaution is worth a pound of cure."

The Clergy

If the preacher would learn the secret of preventing the girl from coming here, he would be applying the "ounce" that would help to cure the evil.

Take the servant girl for instance, the minister and reformer should be invested with authority to investigate her surroundings and expose the conditions found, wherever she is employed. This would be an improvement upon devoting this energy to the welfare of the candidate, or of trying to rescue the girl after her arrival among us.

Observe the hardship this girl must endure who is employed in hotels, note the unsanitary dormitories, and the food with which the servants are supplied, the manner in which the girl is treated by the management, as well as by patrons, and that she is at the mercy of Tom, Dick and Harry; that her environs are such as to be detrimental to her character, and be convinced that those who employ her are most to blame for her downfall.

The servant has no protection; she is a prey for any young man. No matter how

The Underworld Sewer

decently she conducts herself, some young man will find means of communicating with her to lead her wrong; and when it becomes known she is unceremoniously "fired," but the young man is condoned because he is only sowing his wild oats.

The rich people find it difficult to obtain servants at any price; and to keep them is another thing.

WHY HAVE THEY BECOME SO SCARCE? The question is easy to answer, THEY ARE IN THE UNDERWORLD.

Hundreds of girls flow into the sewer every year from those who have been employed by your members.

If the minister would exhort the members of his church to be less indifferent to the comfort and privileges of these girls they would not come to the underworld from everywhere.

The girl who labors for others is often required to sleep in cold corners in winter, and hot garrets in summer, not always free from vermin.

The Clergy

They have no place to receive their company except in the kitchen or upon the street.

These girls who do your washing, cleaning, and cooking, who are earning a respectable living by the "sweat of their brow" are treated as slaves.

These good girls are made to feel that the work they do disqualifies them from being respected, or noticed by friends and visitors of the family.

Is it not true that you believe that public sentiment REQUIRES THAT YOU MAKE YOUR GIRL "KEEP HER PLACE"? The home servant girl, who is of a refined nature, is the one most likely to lose self-respect by reason of the treatment accorded her by the family for which she labors.

She is not taken into consideration at all, except for the work she does; if she proves to be capable she is very much appreciated, but she MUST KEEP HER PLACE.

If it was the custom to put the servant on an equal footing with the family, and com-

The Underworld Sewer

pel the men to KEEP THEIR PLACE; and if the lady of the house would be motherly and friendly to the young girl, there would be but few of them find their way to the underworld.

If the girl who does the work in the family could have the same advantages as the girl she works for, she would not be "our servant," not our "hired girl," but would be introduced as OUR FRIEND; she would be a noble servant, and she would no sooner go forth into the underworld than would the girl she works for. The men of the household, or others, would not dare intrude upon the girl surrounded by such protection.

The clergyman has great influence relating to the management of the homes of his congregation, he has a good opportunity to reach, educate, and uplift his people to a true sense of their duty to their maid servants.

Also to explain to the mothers that by their teaching, or permitting, their boys to believe that the wild oats sowing is inevitable they are unconsciously CONTRIBUTING

The Clergy

TO THE MISERY IN THE UNDER-
WORLD.

You have an opportunity to explain to
the men, both young and old, that it is their
duty to be just as respectful to the other
man's daughter or to the other man's sister
as his own.

You have, no doubt, explained to your
congregation that the only church which is
of any use to humanity is the one carried
in the heart, but the effect is not visible, at
least the servant girl has not been able to
discover it. The good sisters greatest fault
is ignorance of their duty toward those who
labor for them.

The minister delivers a sermon on the subject of unpardonable sin, but he does not
mention where the blame lies, or tell his congregation that nine out of ten of the families
who keep a servant girl TREAT HER IN
A MANNER WHICH TENDS TO
DRIVE HER TO THE UNDER-
WORLD.

The subject is handled so tenderly that
the members imagine that the sermon is only
a diversion, not to be taken seriously.

The Underworld Sewer

If the minister in the pulpit talks too plainly as to the sins of his flock he may be found in search of a new field; but that is not a sufficient excuse to neglect his duty. He must talk openly and broadly of the wickedness, and the methods and conditions which bring girls here. And start the reformation in the homes of the congregation.

If they will do so it will make the world a mighty sight better, and would bring thousands of good people to fight the evil as openly as they are now fighting the liquor evil.

In the absence of a better excuse, the blame for the existence of the underworld is deposited at the door of the fallen women, because, in your blind prejudice, you WILL NOT SEARCH FOR THE REAL CAUSE. This occurs to us as an unreasonable proceeding coming from the most enlightened people of the age.

Driving the women out of town to save the growing up boys was your grandfathers' remedy, and it DOES NOT SEEM TO HAVE IMPROVED THE BOYS,

The Clergy

judging from the gorgeous palaces we have in the underworld.

Who furnished the money to build your great church?

Who furnished the money to build our palaces?

These are questions for those who are interested to determine.

We prefer to believe that the minister is sincere, even though he ceases his interest in us as soon as the election is settled. The candidate and the preacher who were so concerned about the boys suddenly cease to harass us and disappear to settle down in their different vocations; the politician goes to his office, the preacher goes back to the pulpit, and the woman goes back to the underworld, until the next campaign.

The modern way of dealing with our girls is no more humane than the stoning to death of Bible times. If it wasn't so terribly out of date this would be our fate now; but there is the electric gallows; if a few million of us could be put out of our misery by this meansHOW LONG WOULD IT TAKE

The Underworld Sewer

THESE SAVED BOYS, UNDER OUR PRESENT STATE OF CIVILIZATION, TO REPLENISH THE UNDERWORLD WITH JUST AS MANY GIRLS AS WERE THERE PRIOR TO THE ELECTROCUTION?

The accusation by the grand jury, the pulpit, and the politician that we "permit, entice, encourage high school boys and boys of tender age" to come to the underworld is false and ridiculous. They are not wanted and seldom try to come.

In order to DIVERT THE ATTENTION FROM THE FULL GROWN MAN, they talk much and LENGTHY upon the subject of "saving our boys." This is one of the many political tricks, which is used when in search of official glory.

The boys do not support the underworld, which every one knows. But he helps to SUPPLY IT from his big field of wild oats.

If the politician should be punished according to his iniquity and campaign lies, WE SHUDDER TO THINK OF HIS FATE.

The Clergy

There are thousands of dear sweet-faced boys coming to the underworld every day, however, in every town and city. They are employed by the messenger service, telegraph service, and delivery service, ALL OF WHICH NEED OUR PATRONAGE. THEY GLADLY SEND THESE CHILDREN IN ANSWER TO CALLS FROM US at any time. The messenger boys are most to be pitied; they are KEPT CONSTANTLY BUSY DOING ERRANDS FOR MEN AND WOMEN ENGAGED IN DEBAUCHERY.

Men employ them to send communications to girls, and girls employ them to send messages to customers and their lovers.

They are sent to bring lunch, cigars, cigarettes and liquor for a drunken party of men and women, at all times of the day or night, who are clad in the scantiest attire and often none at all.

This drunken bunch joke and use badinage with these boys, such as would be expected to come from a crowd in such a state.

While these boys are timid at first they

The Underworld Sewer

soon learn to give the answer suitable for the occasion in slang and profanity.

The boys are delighted to serve these crowds, because they are supplied with liberal tips, and because they are curious to learn what happens in the underworld. They take up the cigarette habit in no time.

In no other way is there such a chance to see the worst side of the "elephant" and TO BECOME FAMILIAR WITH THE DETAILS OF OUR LIVES, AS TO BE EMPLOYED ON THE MESSENGER FORCE. WHO IS TO BLAME?

The messenger service is depending to a large extent upon our patronage; the reputation surrounding us is well known to all. The ignorant parents permit the small boy to have a schooling that WILL LAST THROUGH LIFE.

EVERY MEMBER OF THE THREE GRAND JURIES OF 1908 WAS AWARE that thousands of boys of "tender age" ARE SENT BY DIFFERENT CORPORATIONS down into the underworld everywhere, WITH FULL

The Clergy

KNOWLEDGE THAT THEY ARE SUBJECTED TO THE GROSSEST CONTAMINATION, but NOT ONE of them RAISED A VOICE RECOMMENDING A LAW TO PREVENT IT.

"Save the boys" does not seem to include service boys, not that they are less important, but it would be a black eye to the corporations to be compelled to provide other means of delivering messages. But all other boys must be removed from the conditions instead of removing the conditions from the boys, which conditions keep the daily press teeming with accounts of our doing.

We certainly must tell the grand jury once more that WE REGARD IT AS A GRAND FARCE. Not to say anything about our private opinion.

If the ministers had been led for a few generations to devote so much energy to prevent boys from growing wild oats, and teaching men to protect and respect women, as he has been in assisting the politician, THOUSANDS OF SOULS WOULD HAVE BEEN SAVED FROM THE

The Underworld Sewer

YAWNING ABYSS OF THE UN-
DERWORLD.

While I may seem to say harsh things of
the preachers, I respect them, and I hope
that I may not be misunderstood, for I believe that they are good men, as a rule, do
good work, BUT THEY MUST
BE JARRED LOOSE FROM THE
USUAL WAY OF TREATING THE
SOCIAL EVIL.

Notwithstanding such conditions, there is
hope which rests upon the possibility that
boys may be taught and men brought to
practice self-control.

CHAPTER XXVI.

Reform and Reformer

Will a woman from the underworld be allowed to reform?

The Christian world is delighted to have a MAN who has been a drunkard, and burdened with all of the sins which go with that condition, reform.

He is encouraged, invited into business circles, into the home, into the church, upon the platform, and into public life. He is not obliged to hide behind false colors.

From him all are eager to learn what course may be best adopted to rescue men from the drunkard's grave, and he is encouraged in that work.

The underworld women who have escaped from the life should have the same encouragement. WHY IS IT NOT TENDERED HER?

The Christian world believe that it is easy

287

The Underworld Sewer

for a woman to reform, that if she has the desire to do so nothing more is necessary.

It is thought that all we have got to do is to pack up, and go where we are not known, cut out all former associates, take employment at good pay, or marry a rich man.

And no matter what inducements are brought to bear to entice us back, all we have to do is to be firm.

If from want and privation we suffer, all we have got to do IS TO BE FIRM.

Showing how meager is the comprehensive views of the real situation.

When the girl or woman leaves the underworld unassisted, it is a most important and difficult step.

It is an easy road to go down, but to go back it is up hill all the way.

From reckless despair she drifted into the life; it is with determination bordering on recklessness that she starts to quit it.

If she attempts this step, from choice and upon her own responsibility, it proves that she is in earnest, and that she deserves great

Reform and Reformer

credit for bravery FOR ATTEMPTING TO FACE THE CHRISTIAN WORLD ALONE.

She finds herself up against a big proposition; while she has dropped one sin she is obliged to adopt others to cover up the one she has renounced. For self-protection she is compelled to misrepresent in order to shield herself from the past.

Civilization has not arrived at such a state that she can go to her neighbor, TELL THE WHOLE STORY AND RECEIVE THE "glad hand" of fellowship. TO ADMIT HER FORMER LIFE WOULD BE TO INVITE SNUBS EVERYWHERE.

Her neighbors would whisper among themselves; they would caution their children not to go near her BECAUSE "SHE HAS BEEN A BAD WOMAN."

The world has never been in the humor to hear the truth. And to shield her from gossip she must of a necessity have a fabrication ready to SATISFY THE CURIOSITY OF THE NEIGHBORHOOD AS

The Underworld Sewer

TO HER BIRTH, RELATIONS AND
FRIENDS, AND HER LIFE EXPE-
RIENCE TO DATE.

It is not possible to tell the truth about
herself and receive the respect which she
knows she is entitled to.

So she manufactures a past for herself,
because her neighbors MUST know all.

And in gratifying the inquisitive neighbor
she is in rebellion with herself. SHE IS
PAYING A BIG PRICE FOR THE
GOOD WILL OF A COMMUNITY.

The Christian religion demands of her that
she be truthful, then she questions if her
present condition is on a higher plan than
her past in the sight of God.

She is conscious of being cowardly and
dishonorable; that she is OBTAINING
GOOD-WILL UNDER FALSE PRE-
TENSES; that she must assume this posi-
tion to the end. IS IT WORTH THE
SACRIFICE?

She becomes dissatisfied in carrying on
this deception in order to be RECOG-
NIZED as a PART OF THE CHRIS-

Reform and Reformer

TIAN WORLD. Is such redemption any redemption at all? Who is to blame?

SHE FINDS THAT THERE IS NO PLACE FOR HER IN THE CHRISTIAN WORLD. And that her attempt at reform is something like jumping from the frying-pan into the fire.

The reformed fallen woman desires to live according to the dictates of her conscience, BY BEING TRUE TO HER OWN CONVICTIONS IN ALL WAYS, and one of the first demands is frankness with her neighbor. This she deems will bring her in harmony with self-respect and divine laws.

To her, reform does not mean merely to take her person out of the mire; but it also devolves upon her to take her mind therefrom, even though there is no longing to return, the mind drifts back to thousands of incidents which seem to extend over miles and miles of experience in all directions.

Every minute of her past holds a secret; they are her unwelcome companions. She must dismiss them and force her thoughts

The Underworld Sewer

into different channels, and obliterate the memory of the past; THIS IS THE TASK OF THE WOMAN WHO REFORMS.

The women who are rescued from the underworld by rescue people and churches are usually those who are at the very bottom, from the effect of "dope," drink and dissipation and disease, or a young girl now and then who is on the verge of the underworld.

The methods adopted to reform fallen women are not only worthless but heartless. When the church societies undertake to REFORM THE WOMEN IT IS IN THAT LOFTY SANCTIMONIOUS MANNER WHICH IS SIMPLY INTOLERABLE to any woman except one ready to die.

I doubt if there is a girl in the underworld (excepting those who have been brought up in the slums) who has not, more than once, tried to reform, either through her own efforts or through that of the reformers, and one out of a hundred may stand the test; in each case she slaved for small wages and was very much in earnest in her efforts.

Reform and Reformer

The men with whom she associated she meets now in the Christian world, who either shun her and caution their wife and daughters against her, or make advances to which she must yield or be exposed.

The underworld women are treated as though they were heathen Chinese, with neither common sense nor sensibility.

You send reformers to us who are ignorant and uneducated; not to say uncleanly in person—that is, the cleanliness which is next to godliness is nowhere visible.

They talk twaddle, and are carried away by their enthusiasm, regardless of reason.

We realize that he or she is inferior to us in intellect, and even in the knowledge of biblical history, the very subject they try to explain.

If they occasionally rescue a few souls, they parade the facts before the public.

They recommend the rescued woman to their friends as a "POOR, LOST CREATURE" whom they have SAVED FROM SHAME, but she must accept the brand.

One is known as a great worker in the res-

The Underworld Sewer

cue cause in proportion to the number of fallen women he or she can find who can be persuaded to come out of the underworld WITH ITS BRAND "RESCUED" PAINTED IN LARGE LETTERS ALL OVER THEM, THERE TO REMAIN FOR LIFE.

And thus the little respect she had for herself fades away. A woman who is sane cannot endure to be advertised as a reformed fallen woman.

The following is an example of a girl that was rescued by the rescuers. They found a home for her in a family as a domestic. She slaved all day, and at night she had the baby to care for. Without any relaxation this girl toiled on. Each day she was reminded by her mistress how fortunate she was in having a home with respectable people who loved her. She bore this burden as long as she could—but—you can guess what became of her.

The reformed man is not reminded of his past life, nor is he required to slave diurnally for a pittance.

Reform and Reformer

I am acquainted with a woman who married a wealthy man and went to New York city to live. After a term of years her husband failed in business and then deserted her. She became very ill and was taken to a hospital. Finally, when she was convalescent, she went to a large church where daily receptions were being held, and where the ladies are arrayed in fine silks and diamonds.

This destitute woman went there in hopes that these good ladies would help her to obtain employment of some kind. But she was told that they "ministered spiritual food only."

The woman came to the underworld, BECAUSE THERE WAS NO FOOD OBTAINABLE ANYWHERE except that OF THE SPIRITUAL KIND.

The ministers and other good people, who go slumming for the purpose of learning of the causes which bring women to the underworld, SELDOM GET THE SECRET, as it BRINGS BACK LOST HOPE AND BITTER PAIN, to them sacred, and which they could not divulge for

The Underworld Sewer

the mere asking to satisfy the inquisitive and prying slummer and customer. Almost every woman has a history of herself framed up which she gives to all meddlers.

Fallen women give the truth as to their downfall and the experience of their life to each other in confidential talks among themselves only.

The minister who goes slumming, and gives out the stories which he has heard along this line to his congregation, for actual facts, deceives himself as well as his good brothers and sisters.

They never tell the reformer, the visitor, the patron, the true history of their first unpardonable sin; it is a rule for us to relate any story which best suits the occasion. A girl may make the mistake of telling facts about herself in the beginning, but she soon tires of gratifying idle curiosity.

YET THESE PATRONS AND REFORMERS WHO LEARN SO LITTLE OF THE REAL SOURCE OF THE CONDITIONS WHICH EXIST IN THE UNDERWORLD ARE THE

Reform and Reformer

PEOPLE WHO ARE DEPENDED
UPON TO GIVE THE INFORMA-
TION UPON WHICH THE REM-
EDY OF THIS EVIL SHALL BE
FOUNDED.

In fact it is only those who have been a
part of this underworld who know the grief
the girl feels in her solitude, and the heart-
ache and disgust she feels while entertaining
the herd, AND WHO HAVE BEEN AT
THE SAME TIME SEEKING FOR
THE REMEDY, WHO ARE CA-
PABLE OF GIVING AN ACCURATE
ACCOUNT, AND FURNISH THE
TRUE HISTORY OF ITS INHAB-
ITANTS, as will disclose WHAT MUST
BE DONE IN ORDER TO ACCOM-
PLISH A REDEMPTION.

Under the present Christian system
of reformation the fallen woman must
be either a HYPOCRITE ALL HER
LIFE, or she must be KNOWN and
"SPOTTED" AS A REFORMED
FALLEN WOMAN.

There is no other alternative for her.

The Underworld Sewer

When we talk among ourselves as to the reasons for not reforming we agree that we must carry on a deception which is unbearable and next to impossible.

But the GIRL WHO LEAVES THE UNDERWORLD BEHIND, whether she likes to do so or not, MUST COVER UP HER PAST HISTORY, or she must go by the way of the church route, to be watched with suspicion, to be preached to and prayed for. She must not be permitted to forget for a moment that she was a lost soul snatched from perdition.

A girl who comes out of the underworld in disguise and lives the "pure and simple life" as near as any human being can, some man recognizes her, he demands favors; she spurns him, but she knows the consequences. She is aware of the price she must pay to purchase the silence of this blackmailer.

The man tells his best friend the girl's story, who in turn tells his wife—well—the whole community is aroused and notified that there is a woman of bad repute in our midst.

Reform and Reformer

Then you will hear such exclamations as the following: "Just think how she has lied to us." "She has pretended to be a woman of good character!" "And to THINK, I was seen talking with her on the street yesterday!" "And to THINK, I introduced her to Mrs. Brown!" "And to THINK, my daughter has been going to her house!" Whereupon SHE IS SNUBBED AND INSULTED IN THE GROSSEST MANNER. The young people are cautioned not to go near her — "THE BRAZEN-FACED HUSSY."

After which the Christian reformer comes to take possession of her polluted soul. BUT SHE HAS GONE BACK BROKEN-HEARTED TO THE UNDER-WORLD. She always had an exalted opinion of the goodness of people outside of our sphere, believing that no unkindness and injustice existed there. HER EXPERIENCE HAS FILLED HER MIND WITH DOUBT, DISDAIN AND DISGUST.

The reformer follows her to the under-

The Underworld Sewer

world. She is told that there is a gentleman down stairs who wishes to see her; he is a preacher, or something, was the description. "Well!" she said, in loud voice, "tell him to scat, get out, vamoose, rouse mit him, or anything else you please. I shall not come down to discuss affairs with him."

He could hear all she said from where he was standing in the corridor. But he sent up another urgent message. "Tell that reformer," she bawled out, "that if I come down, I will tell him in seven different kinds of languages that his DOCTRINE DOES NOT OFFER THE REFUGE AND PROTECTION THAT A GIRL MUST HAVE TO REFORM." God knows that most of us would gladly leave this wretched life, but it is impossible to do so under the present customs, laws and conditions. "Don't I know; haven't I tried it?" "Tell him to go BACK AND SEARCH FOR THE CAUSES, and MEDITATE upon the ETERNAL TRUTH THAT THEY BAR US FROM RESPECTABILITY, as surely AS WE ARE

Reform and Reformer

BARRED FROM HEAVEN." Then she slammed the door of her room shut and locked it. In two minutes there was a rap at the door, and a voice outside saying: "He still insists upon seeing you." Without opening the door the girl said: "Tell him politely to go to the devil." But the other girl did not deliver the message in that way, but said over the banister: "She will not see you, and there is no use to try to make her."

So the man with his good intentions went away. The servant said afterwards that there were tears in his eyes. This girl has been hardened instead of helped by her experience in the Christian world.

It should not be expected that these frail girls can go back to the office and live over again their experience.

Do not expect these girls to go back to your kitchen to do your drudgery, so long as conditions are such that they are sure to be driven out again.

If they had a chance to earn an honest living and be protected and respected, it would be a great step in advancement. But

The Underworld Sewer

they must take the place at lower wages than other girls, and ceaselessly guard their own history, if they get respectable employment.

When men and women in the Christian world shall have permitted the fallen woman the same opportunities which have **ALWAYS BEEN EXTENDED TO THE FALLEN MAN** it will be less difficult for the girl who is struggling to free herself from a repugnant life.

CHAPTER XXVII.

Diseases

I am most desirous above all to inaugurate a war of extermination against a horrible disease, most frequently called SYPHILIS, and is also known by several other names.

I have been interested for years in trying to discover a practical way in which it would be possible to bring before the public a method to overcome this evil, which is destroying the health of the nation.

It is claimed that this disease originates in the underworld, which is not wholly true, as it can be found scattered among all classes.

The underworld is obliged to be on its guard all the time to elude it.

The underworld aver that men spread the disease instead of women.

It has often been asked: "Why should such a disease afflict the human family?"

The Underworld Sewer

More than half the people have not had the training, which conveys to the understanding, that nature works by fixed laws, and it is only by complying with them that life and health is possible. Any violation of nature's laws is visited with punishment in the form of diseases, according to the importance of the law broken. For the transgressor of the sixth commandment this law has reserved the severest punishment, which is a disease that is contagious and loathsome beyond description, and which drains the body of its vitality and brings deep misery.

It is rarely if ever cured. In the majority of cases the patient is "patched up" by powerful medicine, placing the disease in a dormant state which remains so for a few days, a few weeks, a few months, or a few years, according to the amount of drugs the patient is taking.

But when the patient discontinues the medicine the disease will eventually return in some form or other, and will be just as contagious as it was in the beginning. In other words, the disease may lay dormant

Diseases

for five, ten, or twenty years, or even longer, but when it reappears it is as infectious as it was in the first stages, and may be caught by contact when it appears on the surface of the body.

Besides, the blood is poisoned, and whether or not any symptoms of the malady is manifested it will be handed down to posterity to the third and fourth generation.

Our nation is now suffering from the sins of their ancestors. In thousands of instances it will be observed that the ravages of this disease has done its work.

I have witnessed on many occasions handsome young men steeped in this poison, who have married most highly respectable girls. I have used my best endeavor on these occasions to arouse in the young man some conscientiousness regarding the perpetration of this wrong, but my motive in all cases was misconstrued. Laws, not arguments, is the cure for this crime.

Most people who are afflicted with it will only take medicine long enough for the disease to disappear, then they imagine they are

The Underworld Sewer

cured, and it is almost impossible to convince either man or woman that they are permanently afflicted.

This treacherous disease will lurk behind a face with the smoothest and clearest complexion, NOT A TRACE OF IT MAY BE VISIBLE, and yet THIS HIDDEN ENEMY WILL COME OUT OF ITS HIDING PLACE when the conditions are favorable, and be JUST AS POISONOUS AS IT WAS IN THE FIRST STAGES. Men, young and old, will often conceal it until they are almost beyond hope of recovery. Many have come to me for advice when they were on the verge of suicide. Go under the treatment of the most honest physician you know at once is the only advice one can give. Even though we know it seldom cures, yet it is the only way of saving his life. The doctor's medicine will not often cure, but it is much better than the dope of the quacks who advertise the "sure cure."

If the different courses of medicine are faithfully taken, according to prescription,

Diseases

three or four times a day for **THREE OR FOUR YEARS** the disease may be held in check, and may possibly be killed. But by that time the patient will be suffering with rheumatism and dyspepsia and otherwise a total wreck, which is from the effect of the medicine, so the cure is nearly as bad as the disease.

It is a disgrace to the medical profession that it has not, long ago, let the world comprehend the importance of this ailment. It would be more feared and shunned if the true nature of the affliction was realized. The great number who neglect treatment is traceable to ignorance, believing the malady will disappear without remedies; hence the disregard. In some cases it is modesty which prevents the afflicted from consulting a physician. This disease is the cause of a great number of suicides among the different classes of respectability of both sexes. Ill health is given as the reason for these suicides.

It is the worst disease that exists, and is mentioned less than any other, **BECAUSE**

The Underworld Sewer

IT IS OF SUCH A NATURE THAT IT WOULD BE A DISGRACE TO ADMIT HAVING IT, and the good people who know about it only refer to it in a whisper.

The board of health carefully guard and exterminate all infectious diseases except the worst one.

If there is a case of diphtheria in the neighborhood it is quickly quarantined and so with scarlet-fever, yellow-fever, cholera and small-pox. If the bubonic plague is rumored to be near the coast, our government is at once interested, and ready to head it off. These diseases mean death on short notice.

Although the ordinary contagious diseases are under control, the MOST HORRIBLE and the MOST DESTRUCTIVE OF THEM ALL, and which is the promoter of many others, is PERMITTED TO SCATTER ITS FATAL POISON WITHOUT AN ATTEMPT TO PREVENT IT.

It is appalling to observe the indifference

Diseases

of the city, the county, the state, the nation, THAT NO HEED OF THIS SHAME-FUL DISEASE HAS BEEN TAKEN.

I have more than once requested the members of the legislature to present such a bill, covering this subject. I have EVEN OF-FERED TO HAVE THE BILL PRE-PARED.

But in all cases a refusal was their answer, with the explanation that such a bill must come from the MEDICAL FRATER-NITY. The facts are that no one but a doctor would care to take the initiative in the exposure of knowing so much about the disease. Considering the slice of profit which the fraternity derive from this source, perhaps it does not think it can afford to advocate a system of laws that will quarantine this disease.

It is not my purpose to describe this disease with the many names. The medical fraternity will furnish all such information. Your family physician will do so upon request.

But it may be established as a fact that,

The Underworld Sewer

with more than twenty years of observation, THAT I AM FAMILIAR WITH EVERY FEATURE OF IT—the FIRST SYMPTOMS, the PROGRESSION, the REMEDIES USED AND THE RESULTS.

My mission is to urge an extermination, meaning the beginning of an extermination. It may be only a step in that direction this generation, BUT THAT STEP WOULD BE SUCH A BOON.

False modesty does not belong under the rays of the modern limelight, and should not obscure the road to solve a question of such vital importance to the world.

There are laws prohibiting diseased stock from mingling with the healthy stock. Would IT NOT BE POSSIBLE TO DO AS MUCH FOR THE HUMAN FAMILY?

Why should a man or woman afflicted with this disease be granted license to marry.

Every patient so afflicted should be registered, that either sex could look up the record of the other—on the Missouri plan.

Diseases

A LAW SHOULD BE ENACTED IMMEDIATELY TO REACH THIS HORRIBLE DISEASE, REGARDLESS OF THE CLAIM THAT IT WOULD BE AN INFRINGEMENT UPON INDIVIDUAL LIBERTY.

The individual who is afflicted with syphilis should have less right to HIS LIBERTY than the individual WHO IS AFFLICTED WITH SMALL-POX.

It has been said that no law can be made whereby an individual may be compelled to undergo an examination for a private disease, BUT THE GRAND JURY HAS RECENTLY RECOMMENDED SUCH A LAW FOR OUR GIRLS, and THE SAME LAW SHOULD BE MADE TO APPLY TO MEN WHO VISIT THE UNDERWORLD, as well as those who are supposed to be inoculated, BE THEIR STATION HIGH OR LOW.

This disease is NOT MADE LESS OBNOXIOUS and DANGEROUS BY BEING FOUND IN THE MOST SANI-

311

The Underworld Sewer

TARY SURROUNDINGS, and the most refined part of the city.

Had the grand jury recommended a law that would measure out strong punishment for the person who ATTEMPTS to spread the disease THE MUCH-NEEDED FIRST STEP to the extermination would have been ushered in.

There is no neglect that civilization stands for that is more brutal and wicked than the neglect and indifference to this disease.

IT IS OF THE UTMOST IMPORTANCE THAT LAWS BE ENACTED OF THE MOST STRINGENT CHARACTER TO MEET THE RAVAGES OF THIS AFFLICTION. We owe it to the present, as well as to future, generations. IT CONCERNS THE WHOLE RACE.

Has medical science searched among the diseases of the underworld for the cause of tuberculosis? I asked a young physician one day. He assured me that syphilis had nothing to do with tuberculosis.

My argument is that the human system,

Diseases

so saturated with this poison, will MOST LIKELY RETAIN MUCH OF IT IN THE LUNGS AND WILL INVARIA-BLY DO SO IF THERE IS A TEN-DENCY TO WEAKNESS.

I am guided in my statements wholly by close observation of hundreds of cases that have come under my care. My knowledge of the disease may not be called scientific, but if science means a comprehensive infor-mation, or a branch of knowledge that has a certain completeness, THEN MY KNOWLEDGE ON THIS SUBJECT IS SCIENTIFIC and ought to be con-sidered important in the highest degree. I have witnessed many times young people, strong and hardy, of both sexes, after hav-ing been, to all appearance, cured of syphi-litic poisons, that they suddenly succumbed to what the doctor termed tuberculosis, or what used to be called quick consumption.

Such cases, of course, are in the minority, the greater percentage of this poison so prevalent IS CARRIED IN A GREAT, STRONG-LOOKING BODY, and ap-

The Underworld Sewer

pears again in future generations in the form of another kind of tuberculosis or other afflictions. I believe that most victims now suffering with pulmonary consumption to-day is by reason of inherited poisonous taints of this disease.

The world is watching with intense interest the outcome of the battle with tuberculosis by modern science all over our country. Combined with all skill and sanitary knowledge, there has been little or no perceptible improvements so far, and I am bound to confess that I believe that NOT A GREAT DEAL WILL BE ACCOMPLISHED UNTIL SCIENCE STARTS A CAMPAIGN OF EXTERMINATION AGAINST SYPHILITIC POISONS. It will be unnecessary to go back to the woods or "revert back to barbarism" to be cured of any ailment. The race is not suffering from too high a type of civilization, BUT THE SORT THAT REQUIRES REMODELING.

With all of its advancements the race have yet to learn the importance of morality.

Diseases

Every effort available should be brought to bear to prevent and combat the spread of syphilis. IF THE MEDICAL PROFESSION WOULD OPENLY EXPOSE THE MAGNITUDE OF THIS DISEASE, AND ADVOCATE A SYSTEM OF QUARANTINE, this would be an opening to an effectual remedy, and it would be but a short time until PUBLIC SENTIMENT WOULD CALL FOR SUCH LEGISLATION.

If the race can rid itself of this disease MANY OTHERS WILL FOLLOW. And in two or three generations hence diseases of any kind will be unknown.

"LET HER IN"

MAGDALENE

Up to the wicket-gate of heaven,
  Alone and bent with years,
One Magdalene came at last;
  About her (like as tears)
    The darksome dews of evening fell;
    Inside the gate stood Gabriel.

"Woman, what claim hast thou to these
  Celestial courts?" he said.
And Magdalene pierced with shame,
  Shrank back and bowed her head;
    For, toiling thitherward, ah, me,
    'Twas not this face she hoped to see!

But from a tree of living bloom,
  (Whose branches overhang
The very wall of heaven itself)
  Behold, a blackbird sang
    "Oh, Gabriel forget her sin,
    She is so weary, let her in!"

He waited; then again he spake:
  "Woman, why art thou mute?"
And lo—and nearer—sang the bird,
  Like some sweet silver flute,
    "Oh, Gabriel, forget her sin,
    She is so sorry, let her in!"

But the great Angel turned away
  With no relenting word;
And the deep silence gave no sign,
  Save that the gentle bird—
    As one that weepeth—warbled low,
    "Ah, Gabriel, how couldst thou go!"

Yet, as she stood disconsolate,
  Down to the wicket came
One that she knew (oh, love divine!)
  And called her by her name,
    And loosed the gate and threw it wide,
    And Magdalene went inside!

CHAPTER XXVIII.

The Institution

That the underworld woman is not permitted to reform is the firm conviction of all of our people.

This conclusion is forced upon us by the decision of the Christian world, which is that once a woman has fallen she will never reform, and there is no use to try to help her.

If the men, young or old, who come to us in our castles, houses, cribs, or dives, and associate with us in the sin of the underworld, should be disgraced and branded by the Christian and business world, as we are disgraced and branded by the Christian and business world, this would go a long way toward reformation, as the men would try to avoid the disgrace.

Does the Christian man or woman refuse to associate on equal terms with a man who is our associate and supplies the money which keeps your institutions going?

316

The Institution

Does the Christian man or woman stop to consider whether or not the man with whom they daily associate is a man who supports the institution with his money and is our associate in our palaces of sin?

To illustrate, suppose that a woman should be engaged in legitimate business of some kind, and attend to her affairs daily in a most respectful manner, but nightly associate with the men and women of the underworld, would the Christian and business people, men and women transact business with her very long? Would she be welcomed into the church?

Is it not true that men who associate with her in the underworld would even forbid their families to trade with her, or to even recognize her?

Suppose the man who may be engaged in any branch of business would be treated the same as the woman by the Christian and business people under the same conditions, he would either withdraw his patronage from the institution or go out of business.

Do you say that it is not so bad for men

317

The Underworld Sewer

to associate with us in the underworld as it is for us to be there?

We are there because we must have bread. The man is there because he must have pleasure; he has no other necessity for being there; true, if we were not there the men would not come. But we are not permitted to be anywhere else.

It would be one step in the right direction for Christian people to hold the man in disgrace who associates with us in the underworld.

The social evil is the greatest evil belonging to the present generation, and is growing worse. It must be brought to the surface and exposed to view in order that the people may discover and apply the proper remedy, or at least may encourage energy to lay a reliable foundation.

There has been absolutely no advanced step taken relating to the prevention of the social evil, but the same methods are adopted now which have been tried for generations and proven worthless. People of the nation ALMOST UNIVERSALLY BE-

The Institution

LIEVE THAT THE SOCIAL EVIL
CANNOT BE SUPPRESSED, and it is
almost the unanimous opinion that it is A
CONDITION THAT MUST EXIST in
order that the LIVES OF OUR GOOD
GIRLS AND WOMEN MAY BE PRO-
TECTED from the BEASTLY NA-
TURE OF MEN.

A noted writer says that a woman who
would abolish the social evil is visionary, and
that it would be demanding the thing next
to the impossible, and to undertake it would
be worse than egotism. This comes from a
man who has had the floor for, lo, these many
years, and usually knows what he is talking
about, but on this subject his opinion is far
behind the times. In a very brief space of
time there will be more light in the belfry
of this high tower. Occasionally a writer
will suddenly open a side door from which
a glimpse of another region of his mind appears, and which takes him a notch off from
his high perch in the estimation of his readers. It is a dreadful thing to tackle a new
subject. PUBLIC SENTIMENT MAY

The Underworld Sewer

STAND FOR DISAPPROVAL. This is the scarecrow which is apprehended.

It is the custom of some writers to represent our girls as fairies, or beautiful mermaids, basking in the sea, as though their lives were a continual round of bliss. But our girls do not dwell in fairyland, nor is the life they lead a FAIRY TALE, OR A MERMAID MYTH.

We are aware that our existence presents a romantic side to some men, BUT TO US IT IS A HORRIBLE REALITY OF SIN AND SUFFERING.

Plowing the sea of sin is not visionary, except to those who are satisfied with present conditions; all others will observe THE NECESSITY OF DEEP AND CONSTANT PLOWING UNTIL THERE SHALL "BE NO MORE SEA."

No honor or wealth that the earth has to give would be any consideration FOR A WOMAN TO COME FORTH, TO MAKE A PUBLIC CONFESSION OF HER SINS; SHE WOULD DO SO ONLY BECAUSE IT APPEARS TO

The Institution

BE HER DUTY, regardless of the consequences.

Good people think that social evil is a
HUMAN NECESSITY. When I refer
to good people I mean those who are generally recognized as moral or Christian people.
And when I say that good people stand for
the proposition, that the social evil is a necessity, I SIMPLY STATE A TRUTH
which has been the MAIN SUPPORT of
the evil in every age that is reported in history.

Does it take any argument to convince a
reasonable person that so long as the mind is
imbued with the firm conviction that a certain evil is necessary, such a mind can not
entertain a consideration of any plan to
eradicate that evil.

The FIRST BIT OF EDUCATION
NEEDED IN THIS ADVANCED gen-
eration IS TO BE CONVINCED that
THE EVIL is NOT NECESSARY.

I know that many good people do not
realize the importance of the subject. If
you are one of them then you NEED TO

The Underworld Sewer

BE INFORMED as to the AWFUL DISEASES which are COMING TO THE CHILDREN OF EVERY GENERATION in order to AWAKEN YOU TO A SENSE OF YOUR DUTY.

Should you not know of this? Can you ever know the truth of the matter unless you are told?

Who can tell the facts unless it be those who have been in the underworld?

If my statements will not convince you of this fact it will at least cause you to inform yourself further along this line, and you will learn the truth of what I say. ARE YOU WELL ADVISED UPON THE SUBJECT, SO THAT YOU DO NOT NEED ANY MORE INFORMATION? If you knew so much as that, good people, YOU WOULD BE ENGAGED IN THE CAUSE OF OVERCOMING THE EVIL; you would NOT REST CONTENT WITH THE THOUGHT THAT YOU CANNOT DO ANYTHING TO OVERCOME IT.

The underworld can be abolished with

The Institution

proper energy and earnestness. It is not always the OTHER FELLOW which makes it impossible. There are many ways by which men might be restrained from patronizing the underworld. When it shall be discovered that there are no OPPORTUNITIES TO CONCEAL THEIR DEPREDATIONS men will then begin TO CULTIVATE SELF-CONTROL, an important step that must first come to society.

Society is blind to the evil conduct of men who are our support as well as the source of our downfall.

Men in high and low stations in life NEED TO BE EDUCATED TO EXERCISE SELF-RESTRAINT.

Some men "generously" contribute to our support, with intentions of doing a laudable act—to save us from starvation.

They are so familiar with the existence of the underworld, that they regard it as their right to come there, NOT REALIZING THE ENORMITY OF THEIR SINS, and have NO CONCEPTION OF A

The Underworld Sewer

THOUGHT that REAL HELP WOULD BE THAT which would take us out OF THE CONDITION.

Also, all possible effort must be given to the moral training of boys. When the underworld ceases to be a SEWER for the civilized world, it will be at a period when the boys SHALL HAVE BEEN DIVESTED OF THE PRIVILEGE TO SOW THEIR WILD OATS, and understand that they will be HELD RESPONSIBLE BY RESPECTABLE SOCIETY for IMMORAL CONDUCT, with the SAME DEGREE OF CRITICISM AND OSTRACISM AS THE GIRLS.

The child-labor law should be enacted and carried into effect, so there may be no chance to send little boys down into the underworld as messengers, there to see sights, in all kinds of deshabille, and HEAR LANGUAGE WHICH THEY NEVER FORGET. The abhorrence of such inconsideration for the proper care of boys CANNOT BE EXPRESSED ON WHITE PAPER, IN WHITE LANGUAGE.

The Institution

A girl who reads my book can readily see that going to this life BRINGS NOTHING but MISERY AND DEATH.

If a girl could know in advance that, in a very short time after she enters the underworld, she will be miserable beyond measure, as compared with anything she has ever known or heard of; she WILL BE SNUBBED AND INSULTED BY RESPECTABLE PEOPLE, she will be MOST TERRIBLY ILL TREATED BY DRUNKEN MEN, she will be THROWN INTO THE PATROL WAGON, PARADED THROUGH THE STREETS AND LOCKED UP in a DIRTY JAIL; that whenever the politician NEEDS HER MONEY, she WILL BE KICKED AND CUFFED ABOUT BY THE POLICE, and come to the WORST POVERTY AND DEGRADATION KNOWN TO HUMANITY.

If this was known to her, she would carefully avoid any step in this direction.

Who can really know what the underworld

The Underworld Sewer

really is, and WHO CAN TELL THE HIDEOUS TRUTH of the evil, UN-LESS IT SHOULD BE THOSE WHO HAVE BEEN THERE and had the experience?

The woman who has the thought that we have a good time, or an easy time, IS IN GREAT DANGER. And if you hear a man say so, JUST REGARD HIM AS AN ESCAPED LUNATIC.

Girls and women, in your distress, poverty and disappointments, keep your mind filled with the actual fact that the worst step you can take is to YIELD TO THE IN-FLUENCE OF ANY MAN TO TAKE THE FIRST STEP.

While it is true that we have different classes in the underworld, you should know that we must all come to the lowest condition unless we in some manner escape therefrom. ESCAPES ARE RARITIES, and they ARE FEW AND FAR BETWEEN. The only SURE ESCAPE from the underworld IS DEATH. My personal experience with the police, with the courts, with the

The Institution

austere city officials, is the experience of all women in the underworld.

Good people, let the error creep out of your mind that a woman seeks the life because she has degraded tendencies, or that she is of low origin; but rather try to comprehend that she is either so deficient in education as to be unable to earn a living any other way, or she has not shared the same advantages and protection by which you have surrounded your own home, or she is forced into the life from absolute necessity to keep soul and body together.

In either case it is a reflection upon our boasted civilization, that our citizenship is permitted to be so deficient in education, and that men have not sufficiently advanced out of their aboriginal state to render it unnecessary for girls and women to barricade themselves under the protection of their own homes to be safe, and that we have a system of government that drives girls into this most miserable life.

A girl or woman who comes to the underworld institution must undergo a long siege

The Underworld Sewer

of experience before she is able to understand the meaning of the underworld, showing that from the first to the last the business is taught to her. Every step taken is a new lesson. There is drilling and training in vice, from the beginning to the end of her education in the evil institution.

After a year of this life, she turns into one of three channels, either becomes a tough, hardened creature who is always ready to take a part in every kind of depravity, or is stupefied with dope, lovers and more dope. Or else she is awakened to the horrors of her plight and makes every plan to extricate herself therefrom.

When good men and women shall have broadened, and freed their minds of prejudice, and belief that we are the cause of all evil, they will then realize that we are only the result of a brutal condition.

In all history the social evil has never reached the climax where it is today. This will not be comprehended by those who see only the Christian side of life. But if they will investigate, and compare ancient and

The Institution

medieval history with modern facts, they will find that the evil is overwhelmingly greater in its proportion than it has ever been.

Past history of the evil shows that it was degraded beyond description, or it was protected and upheld by the government. During the past ages the underworld was more vicious and less controlled than it is today.

The inhabitants of the modern underworld are better educated and easier to control and regulate than in the past; BUT THE EVIL HAS GROWN WITH THE POPULATION, UNTIL IT NOW INCLUDES MILLIONS OF HUMAN SOULS, and has CULMINATED INTO A GREAT INSTITUTION, which the CHRISTIAN WORLD PRETENDS TO IGNORE, but WHICH IS NEVERTHELESS AN OPTICAL FACT.

This institution is not created by "mean women for the traffic of their sin," but it has a DEEPER MEANING THAN THE SURFACE WOULD INDICATE.

IT MEANS that EVERY TOWN AND CITY HAS THE UNDER-

The Underworld Sewer

WORLD "CORNERED," and THIS CORNER IS OF VAST BENEFIT TO THE BUSINESS AND CHRISTIAN WORLD IN MORE WAYS THAN ONE.

It is a place where MEN CAN INDULGE the LOWEST PROPENSITIES OF THEIR NATURE, AS WELL ALSO, as one of the MOST VALUABLE INSTITUTIONS OF MODERN TIMES TO PUT MONEY INTO CIRCULATION, from which commerce is everywhere benefited.

Our standing army spends its hundreds of thousands of dollars as soon after pay day as the opportunity occurs in riotous living, and the greater part if it PASSES THROUGH THE SOCIAL EVIL INSTITUTION AND BACK INTO THE BUSINESS CHANNELS OF THE CITY. As a BUSINESS PROPOSITION FOR THE CITY THE UNDERWORLD MEANS LARGE PROFIT AND QUICK RETURNS; only POLITICIANS and BUSINESS

The Institution

ESTABLISHMENTS can REALIZE THE EFFECT WHICH THIS IN-STITUTION has upon the VARIOUS BRANCHES OF COMMERCE, but they are NOT FREE TO ADMIT IT.

Good people, are you justified in perpetuating this institution because of the advantages derived from it?

It is asserted that you DARE NOT PUT THE INSTITUTION OUT OF BUSINESS; that the social evil is so NECESSARY FROM A COMMERCIAL STANDPOINT; that TO ABOLISH IT IN YOUR CITY WOULD DESTROY THE BUSINESS INTERESTS and start the GRASS TO GROW UPON THE STREETS.

The United States generously appropriates millions of dollars annually for the aid of unfortunate people in our land, or in foreign lands, that have suffered by reason of some catastrophe.

The states, counties and cities all over the nation supply thousands and hundreds of thousands of dollars for the erection of

The Underworld Sewer

homes and hospitals for the sick and diseased people of various classes. Church societies and rich men and women do the same. WE HAVE NOT HEARD OF ANYTHING OF THIS KIND HAVING BEEN DONE FOR THE UNDERWORLD. But we are in the MIDST of the WORST KIND OF POVERTY, yet no one comes to our relief, because we are "NOT RESPECTABLE AND THEREFORE NOT DESERVING."

True, a few of our women who occupy the palace have made money out of their disgrace; but all of this grandeur dwindles down to the fact that it was acquired by the depravity of men and sorrow of women; it still represents the worst kind of poverty. The women who are in the business for the profit derived from it, are in favor of the present national administration, expressing a fear that "TIMES WOULD BECOME SO DULL UNDER ANY OTHER." Pity and forbearance belong to those who have nothing but money, whether found inside or outside of our province.

The Institution

The national congress, the state legislatures, counties and cities are generous with their laws and ordinances and appropriations, to suppress vice of many kinds, and to prevent the cause and spread of many dangerous diseases, BUT WE HAVE NOT HEARD OF ANYTHING BEING DONE TO SUPPRESS THE SOCIAL EVIL OR TO PREVENT THE CAUSE AND SPREAD OF THE DISEASES WHICH ARE GOING OUT THROUGH THIS CHANNEL AND HANDED DOWN FROM GENERATION TO GENERATION.

There are many appropriations of large sums of money made by congress and state legislatures for LESS WORTHY PURPOSES THAN TO BUILD HOSPITALS AND HOMES FOR THE USE AND BENEFIT OF WOMEN OF THE UNDERWORLD.

The donations of fortunes by philanthropists to establish hospitals and libraries have been of no benefit to the underworld; WE ARE NOT PERMITTED TO ENTER

The Underworld Sewer

THE HOSPITAL, OR TO USE THE FREE LIBRARY ALONG WITH YOUR FAMILY.

There has never been a donation of any kind extended to us. No attention has been paid to our distress by the Christian world, except to offer salvation for our souls, which costs nothing, and WHICH WE DO NOT NEED HALF AS MUCH AS A CHANCE TO PUT INTO USE THE RELIGION WE ALREADY HAVE.

Millions and millions of dollars come to the underworld daily in the United States, and YET WE ARE AS POOR AS JOB'S TURKEY. Everybody is benefited by the money of the underworld except the woman herself.

To undertake to specifically point out what could be done with all of the inhabitants in the underworld, those supported and those in a destitute condition, we are at first overwhelmed by the magnitude of the proposition, and conclude that we can furnish only an outline of the remedy. But as good men and women become interested in the subject,

The Institution

practical ways and means will be developed and adopted by them, which to specify in detail at this time may be condemned.

Certain it is that unless effectual remedies are applied, life in the underworld will be our doom to the end, as COMPARATIVELY FEW OF OUR GIRLS CAN TAKE ADVANTAGE OF THE OPPORTUNITIES FOR REFORM NOW OFFERED THE FALLEN WOMEN.

You are justified in saying that I have practically CONDEMNED ALL THE PRESENT METHODS AND ALLEGED CONTROL OF THE EVIL AS FAILURES, but in so doing I have presented the facts which prove the truth of my contention, that D I F F E R E N T TREATMENT must be given THE WHOLE SUBJECT.

In proportion to the manner that boys and men cease their evil ways, the social evil will be overcome, the effect of which will be a marvelous change for the betterment of the next generation; yet this great endowment to posterity will not materially benefit the inhabitants of the present underworld.

The Underworld Sewer

THE REMEDY FOR US MUST BE OF A LOCAL APPLICATION. It would be in line with other developments TO APPROPRIATE A FUND TO HELP FREE THE DESTITUTE WOMEN FROM THE UNDERWORLD.

If you believe that it is best not to interfere with the "prosperity" of our country, and imagine that the underworld is not in need of assistance, then we should be allowed at least to continue in our misery without any additional hardship.

But should the good people conclude that the time is ripe for the removal of the underworld, AND HAVE DECIDED TO PERMIT US TO REFORM, then it calls for wise preparations for emergencies and possibilities which may arise. A comprehensive view should be taken of our helplessness, AND BE WELL CONSIDERED, as there ARE SEVERAL MILLIONS OF US, and places must be provided and put in condition for the accommodation of such a vast number, WHEN YOU THINK IT IS WORTH WHILE TO

The Institution

SEND US TO A RESPECTABLE PLACE, INSTEAD OF THE JAIL, OR TREAT US WITH KINDNESS INSTEAD OF BRUTALITY. The city, county, state and nation must furnish schools, hospitals and homes, conducted under good management and moral influence, TO WHICH OUR GIRLS MAY GO, and from which THEY MAY GRADUATE TO RESPECTABILITY, AND ABILITY TO SUPPORT THEMSELVES. When the city, county, state or nation undertakes TO DRIVE US FROM THIS LIFE, BY FORCE, BY THE JAIL AND BY STARVATION, without first providing a respectable place for us to go, IT MAKES A BAD MATTER WORSE, AND THE REMEDY BECOMES HEATHENISH. The daughters, sisters and wives of other men have been made outcasts, and robbed of their birthright, the respect and good will of the people in our nation, to which they should be restored, because they are as much entitled to this consideration as most of the men who

The Underworld Sewer

form your society. IS THERE ANY REASON WHY THE MAN WHO PAYS THE WOMAN MONEY TO SEND HER SOUL TO PERDITION SHALL BE RESPECTED, WHILE THE WOMAN WHO FROM NECESSITY ACCEPTS THE DONATION, SHALL GO TO JAIL, OR BE DRIVEN INTO THE DISTRICT?

Try "rounding up" and jailing the men once in a while.

Enact laws which will compel the lover who has lived upon the earnings of a girl, to marry her and support her.

Send the sick, drunkards and dope fiends to the hospital.

Most of the girls and women are PHYSICALLY UNABLE TO PERFORM WORK AND DRUDGERY. This could be made possible only by practice and instruction in the home, WHICH SHOULD BE PROVIDED FOR THEM.

It is regarded as a step in the right direction by the three grand juries of 1908 to have official examinations and treatment for

338

The Institution

the women. We "second the motion," but it must include all men, from all stations in life, who visit the underworld. Official examination for women has been in vogue at different times for generations, but never for MEN.

All doctors should be required to hand in for registration THE NAMES OF ALL MEN AND WOMEN, WHEREVER FOUND, WHO HAVE BEEN AFFLICTED WITH SYPHILIS.

This would be one of the greatest and most effectual preventives, and a great help toward overcoming the social evil, as men would not care to TAKE CHANCES ON C O M P U L S O R Y REGISTRATION.

Had the grand jury recommended some "knock-out drops" for the GENTLEMEN WHO SUPPORT THE UNDERWORLD institution as well as for the VAMPIRES WHO INFEST IT, the underworld would almost have to go out of business, under such a crushing blow.

Shall the unfortunate daughters, sisters

The Underworld Sewer

and wives all over our land who have been consigned to unutterable servitude, be PERMITTED TO BECOME FREE AMERICAN RESPECTABLE CITIZENS, under the PRESENT METHODS OF GOVERNMENT? Or must they continue in their poverty, sin and degradation until the good people SHALL REALIZE THE NEED OF A REVOLUTION, one that will make a general house-cleaning in our nation from top to bottom?

Such an administration would observe that there are SEVERAL MILLIONS of human souls held in captivity by a condition MADE FOR THEM by mildewed laws and customs which keep the UNDERWORLD SEWER GOING.

Good people, I know that you will not readily acknowledge that you stand for keeping the UNDERWORLD going; you may not acknowledge it at all, and still be sincere in your views.

I do not make the assertion that you do so stand as an individual, but YOU CER-

The Institution

TAINLY DO AS A BODY. I have proven this by the public press; by the proceedings of the courts; by the methods promulgated by the city mayor, the police board, the city council, the chief of police, the officer on the beat, the grand jury, the sheriff, and all other officers of the law who have to do with the management of the social evil. They ALL STAND FOR THE PROPOSITION THAT THE EVIL IS AN INSTITUTION THAT MUST BE CONTINUED. The governors and legislatures, the president of the United States, senators and congressmen, ALL STAND FOR THE SAME.

Good people, ARE YOU NOT INDIVIDUALLY RESPONSIBLE ALSO? The village, city, county, state and national officers are selected by you.

You as a citizen are responsible for them. I WANT YOU TO REALIZE THAT THE RESPONSIBILITY RESTS WITH YOU, in order that you may find it to be your duty to help CHANGE THE CONDITIONS.

The Underworld Sewer

Honest people will deny the necessity of the institution, and stand against allowing and upholding it, with or without regulations, AS SOON AS THEY CAN CLEARLY UNDERSTAND THAT THEIR INFLUENCE IS ON THE WRONG SIDE.

When you learn how the underworld is created and exists and what it really is, you will conclude with me, that NO TIME SHOULD BE LOST IN MAKING A STRONG AND UNITED MOVEMENT against its existence.

Printed in the USA
CPSIA information can be obtained
at www.ICGtesting.com
CBHW060116231024
16264CB00004B/184

9 780803 297975